The Man Who Mirrors God's Heart

Finding Reconciliation Beyond Missed Opportunity

Jody Moore

Copyright © 2016 by **Jody Moore**

All rights reserved. No part of this publication may be reproduced, distributed, or transmitted in any form or by any means, without prior written permission.

Unless otherwise noted, all Scripture quotations are taken from the Holman Christian Standard Bible®, Copyright © 1999, 2000, 2002, 2003, 2009 by Holman Bible Publishers. Used by permission. Holman Christian Standard Bible®, Holman CSB®, and HCSB® are federally registered trademarks of Holman Bible Publishers.

The ESV® Bible (The Holy Bible, English Standard Version®) copyright © 2001 by Crossway, a publishing ministry of Good News Publishers. ESV® Text Edition: 2011. The ESV® text has been reproduced in cooperation with and by permission of Good News Publishers. Unauthorized reproduction of this publication is prohibited. All rights reserved.

Scripture quotations marked (NCV) are taken from the New Century Version®. Copyright © 2005 by Thomas Nelson. Used by permission. All rights reserved.

Scripture quotations marked (NIV) are taken from the Holy Bible, New International Version. Copyright © 1973, 1978, 1984 by the International Bible Society. Used by permission of the International Bible Society.

Sermon To Book
www.sermontobook.com

The Man Who Mirrors God's Heart / Jody Moore
ISBN-13: 9780692728635
ISBN-10: 0692728635

GOD'S WILL > YOUR PLAN

God has a plan and a purpose
—and you are a part of it!

Discover what the story of Jonah can teach you about embracing your call, purpose, and identity.

I dedicate this book to my fathers:

To my biological father, Roland Moore, who gave me life and loved me.

To Ronald Lowe, the man who led me to the Lord at age nine. You became my father in the faith. I am eternally grateful.

To my uncle Walter Dupree, who modeled manhood to me at an early age and allowed me a front-row seat to his life as he raised his son.

To my uncle, Dr. Melvin Jetter, the man who looked after me and took care of me when my father could not.

To Dr. Larry Titus, who became a father in ministry to me and was my inspiration for launching Praise Tabernacle Bible Church.

To my father-in-law, Bishop Kenneth Ulmer. You have loved me as a son and have afforded me a wide space to grow and become a man worthy of your daughter. Thank you for covering me and showing me what it means to be a caring father.

Acknowledgements

God has blessed me with so many people who have mentored and supported me in my journey.

I am always grateful for my mother, Janice Moore, who as a single mother had to step into the role of a father many times. She kept me wrapped in the *ornament of grace*.

I recognize the many people who have mentored me: Charles Powers (deceased), my mentor in middle school gave me a love for history and learning. Dr. Charlene Taylor Evans of Texas Southern University gave me a love for literature; she opened her home to me and fed me while I was a struggling undergrad. Kathleen Johnston and John Foss, both senior executives from my corporate life, mentored me and taught me how to navigate through the world of executive leadership in a Fortune 500 company.

I am also forever grateful for the wonderful people whom I have been privileged to shepherd for over thirteen years. Praise Tabernacle, you are an amazing people whom I have watched grow into a powerhouse of love, worship, and passion for the glory of God. I love you all.

I journey in life with some amazing brothers. Thank you, Pastors Bryan Loritts, Deandre Salter, and Wayne Chaney, for locking arms with me on this journey.

I want to thank my "Inland Empire" friends who encourage me to serve in this part of the vineyard: Pastor Kelvin Simmons (Immanuel Praise), Dr. Joshua Beckley (Ecclesia Fellowship), and Pastor Mike Spradlin (Valley Christian)—I thank you for allowing me to hang out with you!

There are a few men in particular who have allowed me into their lives. Some call me a "spiritual father" while others just allow me to impart a little wisdom (run my mouth) from time to time over coffee. To Pastor Kevin Henderson (Praise Tab), Pastor Sam Casey (New Life), Pastor Russell Lewis (Covenant Life), Pastor Jim Cutter (Regency), and Kelvin Washington: please know that I have learned as much from you as you have from me. Let the Iron Sharpening continue! I am grateful.

To all the men with whom I have walked in discipleship on Thursday nights: thank you for allowing me to pour into you and for allowing me the privilege of walking with you into maturity as men of God.

To my children—Marcquel, Kamryn, Raegan, and Bailee Moore—I live for you all. I pray that you will look back in life and see me as a father who you can say loved you and of whom you are proud.

Keniya Moore, the wife of my youth, you are an amazing woman. God knew what He was doing when He hooked us up at Starbucks over 17 years ago. If grace is when we get from God what we do not deserve, then you are the manifestation of God's grace in my life.

CONTENTS

Note from the Author 3
Mirroring the Heart of God 5
Humility Propels Us Forward 9
Missed Opportunities of Fatherhood 43
The Power of Authentic Reconciliation 83
Grace to Move Forward 117
About the Author 120
About Sermon To Book 122

WELCOME

Note from the Author

Thank you for purchasing *The Man Who Mirrors God's Heart*!

Accompanying each main chapter of the book is a set of reflective questions with a practical, application-oriented action step. These workbook sections are a tool to help you delve deeper and connect the lessons of David's life to your own experiences as a believer, spouse, and parent.

I recommend you go through these workbook sections with a pen in order to write your thoughts and record notes in the areas provided. The questions are suitable for independent reflection, discussion with a friend, or review with a study group.

Regardless of what led you to this book or how you choose to approach it, I hope that the experience of reading and reflecting on it helps you understand more fully what qualities bring us closer to the heart of God.

INTRODUCTION

Mirroring the Heart of God

Our purpose in studying the life of a well-known biblical character is to see how God works in the lives of others and how they respond to him. But of all the historical figures we could learn about, why David?

David was considered by most theologians to be the most successful king who ever lived, although he was neither the richest nor the wisest. That accolade would go to his son, Solomon. David's life began what we call the messianic line. That is, his lineage led to Jesus Christ. Actually, the messianic line went back even further. It actually started with Adam, as Luke pointed out when he recorded the genealogy. But the messianic line as it related to *kingship* began with King David.

David was born to a man named Jesse. We know little to nothing about his mother, but we know Jesse was the grandson of Boaz and Ruth, and our text describes him as a Bethlehemite.

David was considered to be a man after God's own heart. He was an effective leader, administrator, and shepherd, one who was mightily used by God. In the midst of all this, though, he stumbled and made some serious mistakes. His mistakes, missed opportunities, and weaknesses were a prominent part of his life. How can someone who began as a lowly, humble shepherd favored by God end up being a mighty king who nearly falls from grace?

God will do some amazing things through many of us, things that will have a direct effect on the advancement of His kingdom.

If you've ever made mistakes, you're a good candidate to be successful. David succeeded in spite of his missteps, and there were more than one. He is most known for the sins of adultery and murder he committed with Bathsheba, but he made several other mistakes during his lifetime as well.

Again, why should we study David? I believe that God will do some amazing things through many of us, things that will have a direct effect on the advancement of His kingdom. We're going to examine the life of a man who did great things as a result of his heart being focused in the right direction.

As we read about why God favored David's humility, we will see that to be people after God's own heart, we must obey God, actively engage with our families, and have a heart for authentic reconciliation with God and others.

Like David, we too will see limitless grace on our lives to do certain things for the kingdom. But it will only happen for us if we become living reflections of God's heart.

CHAPTER ONE

Humility Propels Us Forward

To understand how David's unexpected journey began, we must first look in the sixteenth chapter of 1 Samuel:

> The LORD said to Samuel, "How long are you going to mourn for Saul, since I have rejected him from being king over Israel? Fill your horn with oil, and go. I am sending you to Jesse of Bethlehem because I have selected a king from his sons." Samuel asked, "How can I go? Saul will hear about it and kill me!" The LORD answered, "Take a young cow with you and say, 'I have come to sacrifice to the LORD.'
>
> Then invite Jesse to the sacrifice, and I will let you know what you are to do. You are to anoint for Me the one I indicate to you. Samuel did what the LORD directed and went to Bethlehem. When the elders of the town met him, trembled and asked, "Do you come in peace?" "In peace," he replied. I've come to sacrifice to the LORD. Consecrate yourselves and come with me to the sacrifice. Then he consecrated Jesse and his sons and invited them to the sacrifice.
>
> When they arrived, Samuel saw Eliab and said, "Certainly the LORD's anointed one is here before Him." But the LORD said to Samuel, "Do not look at his appearance or his stature, because I

> have rejected him. Man does not see what the LORD see, for man sees what is visible, but the LORD sees the heart." Jesse called Abinadab and presented him to Samuel. The LORD hasn't chosen this one either." Samuel said. Then Jesse presented Shammah, but Samuel said, "The LORD hasn't chosen this one either." After Jesse presented seven of his sons to him, Samuel told Jesse, "The LORD hasn't chosen any these." Samuel asked him, "Are these all the sons you have?" 'There is still the youngest," he answered, "but right now he's tending the sheep." Samuel told Jesse, "Send for him. We won't sit down to eat until he gets here."
>
> So Jesse sent for him. He had beautiful eyes and a healthy, handsome appearance. Then the LORD said, "Anoint him, for he is the one." So Samuel took the horn of oil, anointed him in the presence of his brothers, and the Spirit of the LORD took control of David from that day forward. Then Samuel set out and went to Ramah. — **1 Samuel 16:1-13**

Samuel had the task of locating the new king God had chosen. If we go back to chapter 13, we see the rejection of Saul, who was king over Israel. God has told Samuel he is pretty much done with Saul. "But now your kingdom shall will not endure; the Lord has sought out a man after his own heart…" (1 Samuel 13:14 NIV).

So God's kingdom would begin to be established under the rule of David, a rule that would actually continue into the millennial period. But it could only happen with a man with the humility of a shepherd—a man after our Shepherd's own heart.

A Disobedient King

While a young, humble shepherd was busy tending his flock, he was oblivious to the strife, greed, and disobedience happening far away that would eventually affect him. But what brought about the need for God to send Samuel out to find the next king—the one whom God favored?

Sometimes we're so busy looking somewhere else that we miss what God is already doing in our lives.

Our present chapter in Samuel picks up during a period of national transition. Israel had wanted a king because they wanted to be like other nations. They wanted a leader who would go out and fight for them. Never mind that God had been doing this all along. Sometimes we're so busy looking somewhere else that we miss what God is already doing in our lives.

God reluctantly granted their wish, as we see in 1 Samuel 8. Samuel was disappointed in their disloyalty. But God said, in effect, "Don't worry about it, Samuel. This is not about you. They are not rejecting you; they're rejecting me as their king. But look, since they want a king so badly, give them what they want." Little did they know that God had already planned to give them a king later on, King Jesus!

Well, Saul, the people's choice, made two big mistakes. The first was when he was about to go into battle. Before that happened, he knew a sacrifice needed to be offered before the Lord. There's an application here. Before you enter a spiritual battle, remember that warfare starts with worship.

So the Israelites needed to worship and sacrifice before going into battle. But there is order in God's kingdom. Saul might have been the king, but only Samuel the prophet could do the sacrifice. Saul had no authority, even as king, to do that. But in his impatience to go into battle, he decided to do the sacrifice himself. God seemed to say, "I can't believe you'd do something like this!"

Disobedience always gets us in the end.

Right then God saw that Saul was his own boss, and was not about to listen. And right then God began to reject him as king.

Secondly, God instructed Saul to wipe out all the Amalekites. He was not to leave one Amalekite alive. So Saul went out to battle, and won. And once again, he did his own thing. He decided to keep the king alive, as well as the best sheep and goats.

"But I did what you told me to do," Saul protested to the Lord in his own defense. "I just kept the king and the sheep; I kept the best stuff to make sacrifices to you with."

In other words, he was going to make it about God. But that was not what God had told him to do. Partial or delayed obedience was still disobedience. So God said, "I've rejected Saul from being king." And Samuel was to announce it to him. The two met and the message was delivered.

Are we enjoying a pity party right now, and playing the victim over someone or something God is finished with?

When Samuel turned around to leave, however, Saul fell and grabbed the hem of his garment, causing it to tear. "That's the sign God has now torn the kingdom from your hand," Samuel told him. Disobedience always gets us in the end. Saul himself was later killed by an Amalekite.

> The LORD said to Samuel, "How long are you going to mourn for Saul, since I have rejected him as king over Israel?' — **1 Samuel 16:1**

Samuel is clearly hurting. The words "I have rejected" in the Hebrew are suggestive of completed action. What God was saying, in effect, was, "I'm finished with Saul. I am moving into a new season, Samuel, but you are still crying over the old one! No mourning is ever going to fix this. So why don't you get back up? Stop crying and move into the new thing I have for you."

Submitting to God's Way Forward

We all need to tune ourselves in to the moves of God and stop trying to hold on to something He is finished with. Are we like Samuel enjoying a pity party right now, and playing the victim over someone or something God is finished with? Could it be time to stop living in the past and move into the next season? Our pain may be real, but at some point, we need to stop talking about what somebody once did to us.

Many of us are still waiting for action from God when He may have already done something—we just haven't gotten the word yet.

I hear it all the time when I counsel people.
"But they did this!"
"I know. You've told me."
"But Pastor she did this!"
"I know. You've told me."
"But Pastor, you don't know what they did to me on the job."
"Yes I do, because you've told me five times!"
God would say, "I'm tired of hearing it. That thing is over. How long are you going to keep bellyaching? Get yourself up, and move into a new season."
Now look at the instructions God gave to Samuel. He said, "Fill your horn with oil. Go where I'm sending you.

I have provided a king for myself." The Hebrew verb again suggests a sense of completion. God was saying, "It's done. I've already completed the search process. Recruitment is finished. No more interviews. I have already chosen a king for myself."

So the job was done, although David didn't know about it yet. Many of us are still waiting for action from God when He may have already done something—we just haven't got the word yet.

When God tells us to go somewhere, we had better get over our fear and go.

In verses 2 to 5 of 1 Samuel 16, Samuel told God he was scared Saul would take him out if he started announcing that somebody else was going to be king.

God said, "Go anyway."

When God tells us to go somewhere, we had better get over our fear and go. We must not worry about what might happen, or how we might look.

"Here's what you have to do," God told Samuel. "Go under the guise of sacrifice. Take up a heifer and say you're going to sacrifice to the Lord. Then go and consecrate Jesse's sons."

When Samuel reached the town the elders saw him coming and got worried. He had so much authority on his life that as soon as he stepped into a city the elders began to tremble. They asked whether he came in peace.

> "In peace," he replied. "I've come to sacrifice to the Lord. Consecrate yourselves and come with me to the sacrifice." Then he consecrated Jesse and his sons and invited them to the sacrifice. — **1 Samuel 16:5**

God's choosing of David to be the king gives us a glimpse of His decision-making process. He does not choose progressively as we do. He doesn't see what's happening and then make a choice. Because God is omniscient, He knows the end from the beginning.

God's method of choosing is far different from ours.

For us human beings, it's different. We choose at the beginning of each day what we will do and what we will wear. But God doesn't make choices in time. He decrees one choice, and that choice is acted out *over* time. God doesn't decide tomorrow that somebody's going to be born. He didn't decide, nine months before October 14, 1968 that Jody Moore was going to be born on that date. He decreed it once in eternity, and by God's hand of providence it came to pass on October 14, 1968.

So when God said, "I've chosen David as king," He didn't just scratch his head after Saul and say, "Oh I think David might be a good choice." David was chosen before time began. We can see that God's method of choosing is far different from ours.

In verse 5 of chapter 16, Samuel consecrated Jesse and his sons and invited them to the sacrifice. When they arrived, he looked at Eliab and thought, *Surely the Lord's anointed is standing here before the Lord.*

But the LORD said to Samuel, "Do not look on his appearance or on the height of his stature, because I have rejected him. For the LORD sees not as man sees: man looks on the outward appearance, but the LORD looks on the heart" (1 Samuel 16:7 ESV).

It's as if God were saying, "You've already been there and done that and it didn't work."

As great a prophet as Samuel was, he still could only make choices based on his human limitations. He saw Eliab and immediately assumed he must be the one, evidently by his height.

> Samuel had all the tribes of Israel come forward, and the tribe of Benjamin was selected. Then he had the tribe of Benjamin come forward by its clans, and the Matrite clan was selected. Finally, Saul son of Kish was selected. But when they searched for him, they could not find him. They again inquired of the LORD, "Has the man come here yet?" The LORD replied, "There he is, hidden among the supplies."
>
> They ran and got him from there. When he stood among the people, he stood taller than anyone else. Samuel said to all the people, "Do you see the one the LORD has chosen? There is no one like him among the entire population." And all the people shouted, "Long live the king!" — **1 Samuel 10:20-24**

In chapter 16, the Lord told Samuel he was *not* to choose Eliab because of how he looked, but we do know he was tall. It's as if God were saying, "You've already been there and done that and it didn't work."

We need to submit ourselves in humility to what God wants for us—not just something that looks good.

Saul himself was head and shoulders above everybody else. So when Samuel was involved in choosing the next king he felt sure that Eliab, being the tall one, would be the Lord's anointed.

Living Life Vertically

I believe God is telling us we have to go beyond external appearances. We need to submit ourselves in humility to what God wants for us—not just something that looks good. Something may look right and have all the features and stuff we want. It might appear to be just what we're looking for. But we've been there before, and it didn't work out.

Israel had their tall king and it didn't work out. They had someone with height but no depth.

Today are you still hurting over another? He sure did look good didn't he? He sure did talk well didn't he? He sure drove a nice car and dressed nicely, didn't he? And he sure had a good job.

But you chose him based on external factors. God tells us we have to go beyond the surface in our decision-making. If we're not careful the enemy will have us so distracted that we'll spend all of our time and energy on something that looks right but isn't from God.

God is trying to do a quick work in your life, but He can't if you keep lingering on what He's already said no to.

Grandma used to say, "All that glitters ain't gold." The only way we know gold is real is by testing it in the fire. That's why we don't walk away from relationships so fast. Especially if we're married.

Look at verse 7 again. "I have rejected him." Again we find that indication of completed action. God is saying, "Move on from that one. He's not the one. No matter how much you try to clean him up he's still not the one. No matter how much you try to pray her into being the one, she's not the one. I've already rejected her."

Why are you wasting your time? Move on! God is trying to do a quick work in your life, but He can't if you keep lingering on what He's already said no to. He may be saying, "I'm trying to do it, but you're always talking about how slow I am. You keep getting in the way by holding on to something I've already rejected."

In verse 7, God makes it clear that He is different from Samuel who made choices based on outward appearances. Our human limitations restrict our decision-making ability. We cannot see what God sees. But what starts out as limited becomes limitless when we totally depend on God.

> The LORD God took the man and placed him in the garden of Eden to work it and watch over it. And the LORD God commanded the man, "You are free to eat from any tree of the garden, but you must not eat from the tree of the knowledge of good and evil, for on the day you eat from it, you will certainly die.' — **Genesis 2:15-17**

So Adam heard God's commands clearly.

> Now the serpent was the most cunning of all the wild animals that the LORD God had made. He said to the woman, "Did God really say, 'You can't eat from any tree in the garden?' The woman said to the serpent, 'We may eat the fruit from the trees in the middle of the garden, God said, 'You must not eat it or touch it, or you will die.'" "No! You will not die," the serpent said to the woman. "In fact, God knows that when you eat it your eyes will be opened and you will be like God, knowing good and evil." — **Genesis 3:1-5**

> Then the woman saw that the tree was good for food and delightful to look at, and that it was desirable for obtaining wisdom. So she took some of its fruit and ate it; she also gave some to her husband, who was with her, and he ate it. Then the eyes of both of them were opened... — **Genesis 3:6**

The enemy got Eve to make a choice based on *what looked good*. We have said that in our human limitations we tend to make decisions based upon what we see. Here the enemy is exploiting Eve's human limitations. She didn't have to fall for it, however, because she had heard God's voice, and God had told her not to eat the fruit.

We had better learn how to run when we hear what God is speaking into our life.

We always test what we see by what God has told us. We use what we hear from God as a check on what we see in our flesh. In other words, Eve, it didn't matter what the serpent showed you when you knew what God told you.

Are we prepared to say no to something, even though it looks good to us, if it does not line up with what God is telling us? We had better learn how to run when we hear what God is speaking into our life.

Yahweh looks at the heart. The Hebrew word for heart is *leb*. It speaks of our conscience, our emotions, our thoughts, our volitions, and our motives. Only God can see what drives and motivates us. We may see someone who does and says all the right things but only God knows if he says and does these things just to get the attention and affirmation of another person. Only God knows if she's doing what she's doing just to get a pat on the head.

Sometimes we do the right stuff for the wrong reasons. If so, we're not doing it to the glory of God. We need to do what is right because it's pleasing to God, whether or not it's pleasing to anybody else.

God may allow us through His gifting and empowerment to partially see what He sees. This is through the forgotten gift of *discernment*. We love the gifts of tongues and prophecy. But I believe that in this season God is telling us we need discernment.

You can't depend on yourself to be wise, because you can only make decisions based upon sight.

"You need to hear from me," He says. "You need to be walking by revelation. You need to be able to discern intentions and motives. I will show you his or her heart. I will show you what you need to do in this situation. You can't depend on yourself to be wise, because you can only make decisions based upon sight."

We need to live our lives from a vertical perspective, based on what God shows us. We follow the pattern of Jesus when we do that, because Jesus said, "I only do what I see my Father doing."

Our biggest problem is that we keep trying to reinvent the wheel. We try to live our lives according to our personal architecture and design when God is saying, "I've already laid out the pattern for you to walk in towards your destiny. You have to depend on me to reveal that pattern to you."

Too often we live our life from a horizontal perspective. We're driven by what man says and by what we see our neighbor doing. God is saying it's time for us to stop looking at the Joneses. He will fix our horizontal relationships if we live from a vertical perspective.

We need to seek God in humility as Jesus sought after His Father.

The Bible says Jesus had favor with God and favor with man. The first translates into the second. So we need to stop trying to get the favor of man without first getting the favor of God. We need to seek God in humility as Jesus sought after His Father.

An Unlikely King

Remember, Samuel thought Eliab must surely be the anointed one. But the Lord told Samuel not to look on outward appearance. David had favor with God.

> *Jesse called Abinadab and presented him to Samuel. "The LORD hasn't chosen this one either," Samuel said. Then Jesse presented Shammah, but Samuel said, "The LORD hasn't chosen this one either." — 1 Samuel 16:8-9*

How does God choose? By looking at the heart. He often chooses the least likely and the least expected. In 1 Samuel 16:10, Jesse made seven of his sons pass before Samuel, but Samuel said to him, "The Lord has not chosen these." So he asked Jesse, "Are these all the sons you have?"

"There is still the youngest," Jesse answered, "but he is tending the sheep."

In other words, there was somebody else out there, but Jesse didn't bother to bring him to the party. Even Jesse had counted David out from the parade of potentials to go before Samuel.

The person of whom we think little may be the person through whom God has chosen to do great things.

In that culture, the eldest son received the favor and privilege. And David was the youngest of Jesse's sons. Notice that the text says he paraded all seven, but only three of the seven are named. Those three represented the whole seven. So the text implies all of the sons were paraded before Samuel, but the youngest was still out on the field. David was an afterthought.

Be careful whom you overlook! Here was God preparing to raise David up to deliver Israel, while his own daddy was tossing him aside. The person of whom we think little may be the person through whom God has chosen to do great things.

At times the person closest to us can't see the potential within us. This is why, later on, David would say, "When my mother and father forsake me..."

We parents should be careful not to sell our children short of their God-given potential just because they're in a particular season. Our prayer should be, "Lord, let me see my child the way you see my child." That way we're not speaking something into our child's life that is not in alignment with God's purpose for them.

We need to learn how to glorify and honor God in whatever season we are in.

Not only does God choose the least likely, but He'll pull them from the least likely place. Again, verse 11 says, "There is still the youngest, but he is tending the sheep."

Note that Jesse and all of his sons were invited to the feast, at Samuel's request. But Jesse was not interested in including David. God had chosen David for the palace, but he was still in the sheepfold. God had spoken and decreed the palace over David while he was still working in obscurity. Herein lies the tension of living out God's purpose for our life. How often we get frustrated with our present day experience only because we have yet to grab hold of the spoken promise of the palace.

At least David didn't *know* God had spoken palace over his life, so he was content to be out there watching the sheep. In his mind, he was content and this was as good as it was going to get. But what do we do when we know God has declared something over our life that is different from what we are experiencing right now? We need to learn how to glorify and honor God in whatever season we are in. We need to say, "I'm in a rough season but I'm going to praise God anyway." Our attitudes and actions we display when handling the sheepfold is a good indication of how we'll handle things when we finally get to the palace.

Stop thinking it's too late for you. Stop allowing the enemy to get into your head.

In the natural there would appear to be a great distance between where we are now and our final destination. But in God's economy it's always a straight line from the sheepfold to the palace. Our destiny is reachable from whatever starting point we currently find ourselves in. Isn't it just like God to visit someone tending sheep and tell them he has prepared for them to go to the palace?

Our destiny is not always obvious to us, and the enemy wants to get us stuck in the sheepfold and never hear the voice of God promising to take us into the palace. Friends, stop thinking it's too late for you. Stop allowing the enemy to get into your head.

> Samuel asked him, "Are these all the sons you have?" "There is still the youngest, he answered, "but right now he's tending the sheep."

Samuel told Jesse, "Send for him. We won't sit down to eat until he gets here." — 1 Samuel 16:11

The Message Bible puts it like this: "Go get him. We're not moving from this spot until he's here!"

That is the best translation from the original Hebrew. There may be something specific that God wants to do through us, and He is willing to hold things up until we arrive. So we can stop worrying about the time.

God may have an assignment for us, and He has used everything in our lives to fashion us for it.

In this season we are to do what we're supposed to do. This doesn't invite us to laziness or to procrastination. Rather, it invites us into the knowledge that there's something God wants to do through us and He is willing to wait until we get ourselves into position.

Are we aware of what God is calling us to? We know God has spoken to us and yet we object. We might say, "I've made some mistakes. I've screwed up to the point where life seems to have gotten ahead of me."

But God is saying, "Don't dwell on your screw-ups. I have separated you from your sins as far as the east is from the west, and I'm going to give you a chance to catch up. So stop wallowing in self-pity. Get yourself up and begin to move into position."

God may have an assignment for us that He's placed our name beside. And it is so major that He has used all the stuff in our lives to fashion us for it.

"Don't you know," He may be telling us, "that all the hell that you been through has been me fashioning you? I've been setting you up to be used by me!"

God chooses a person because of their heart—not their outside appearance.

When God chooses He also informs. God informed Samuel that David was the chosen one.

> *So [Jesse] sent for [David]. He was glowing with health and had a fine appearance and handsome features. Then the* LORD *said, "Rise and anoint him; this is the one."* — **1 Samuel 16:12 (NIV)**

In verse 12, Samuel heard the voice of God in his spirit. God was giving him confirmation that David was the one to anoint. Notice that God was saying this to someone *other* than David or David's father. When God is moving in your life, He will often confirm it through someone else.

So whom does God choose? The person who is least likely, or someone we probably wouldn't choose if it were up to us. God chooses a person because of their heart—not their outside appearance.

The Power of God's Anointing

> So Samuel took the horn of oil and anointed him in the presence of his brothers, and from that day on the Spirit of the LORD came powerfully upon David. Samuel then went to Ramah. — **1 Samuel 16:13 (NIV)**

Here, for the first time in Scripture, the name David is mentioned. All through Scripture, people's names are repeated. But there was only one David. There might have been others, but none are recorded in the Bible. The name means "beloved."

The Spirit's flow was ongoing. Even when David messed up, he would not lose that anointing.

The anointing of David by Samuel meant God had set David apart for a special assignment. But it also meant God had equipped and empowered him to fulfill it.

The New International Version says that the Spirit *came powerfully* upon him. And the Message translation says that the Spirit *entered* David. The word translated "came powerfully" is in the imperfect in Hebrew, which meant the action was ongoing. So the Spirit's flow was ongoing. There would now be a season of continual anointing on David. And even when he messed up, he would not lose that anointing.

Note that Samuel anointed David in the company of his brothers. He had looked at Jesse's oldest son and thought to himself that Eliab must be the one. But God rejected Eliab. Two more sons appeared before Samuel but they weren't the right ones either. Samuel, knowing something was wrong then asked Jesse if there were other sons. Here David entered the picture.

We should not assume that just because God has started to move in our life, the people around us will understand what God is up to.

God affirmed to Samuel that David was the one and instructed him to anoint him. Remember, the only one who knew that God was looking for another king was Samuel. He had told nobody the real reason for his visit but just said he was there to sacrifice. So David was now being anointed by the great prophet while his brothers, who technically should have been first in line, were standing around him in a circle. Not one time does the narrator ever disclose why Samuel was there. As far as we can tell from the text, neither Jesse nor his sons knew what was happening or what it meant.

We should not assume that just because God has started to move in our life, the people around us will understand what God is up to. In fact, they may never get what God is up to in our life. We see this in 1 Samuel 17, where David is about to take on Goliath.

> *David spoke to the men who were standing with him: "What will be done for the man who kills that Philistine and removes this disgrace from Israel? Just who is this uncircumcised Philistine that he should defy the armies of the living God?"* — **1 Samuel 17:26**

The people told him what would be done for the man who killed the giant, and Eliab—David's eldest brother—overheard the conversation and was furious.

People will try to define us based on where we are today. But we need to say, "My epilogue is looking different from my prologue."

"Why have you come down here?" "And with whom did you leave those few sheep in the wilderness? I know how conceited you are and how wicked your heart is; you came down only to watch the battle" (1 Samuel 17:28 NIV).

Remember, David had been anointed in front of Eliab, and God was at work in David's life. But even though Eliab had a close view of what was happening, he still didn't get it. Transition had already started in David's life and his own family couldn't see it.

There will be people in your life who can never transition with you from the sheepfold to the palace because all they see is sheepfold material. "Why aren't you tending those sheep?" Eliab sneers at David.

People will try to define us. They will try to project onto us a destiny based on where we are today. But we need to get to the place where we can say, "My epilogue is looking different from my prologue."

We'll never hear God's voice calling us to the palace when all we can hear is the voice telling us to stay with the sheep.

If you read further through the book of 1 Samuel, you'll find that David's brothers were never close to him during his transition to kingship. David would become best friends with Jonathan, who was not even his relative. Why do you suppose this was? It was because David's brothers could never accept what God was doing in his life. But when God is superintending the transition, it doesn't matter who gets it and who doesn't.

We can slow down our progress if we try to explain what God is doing in our life to some people. But if someone is truly a part of our life by way of brotherhood, sisterhood or friendship, they ought to be able to discern when God's hand is on us and not only celebrate with us but also guide us forward.

We must not be so codependent on certain relationships that we're willing to hold on to them at any cost. This is because our important relationships define who we are. And if someone sees us only in the sheepfold then that's how we may see ourselves as well. We'll never hear God's voice calling us to the palace when all we can hear is the voice telling us to stay with the sheep.

David was on assignment, not just from God but from his natural father. Jesse sent him out there with food for the very ones who were talking about him. We need to take care we don't discount who God may be sending to bless our lives. Jesse sent David out there with food for his brothers, and they complained, "What are you doing out here? Who's looking after those sheep?" (1 Samuel 17:17-18, 28).

We might not be see ourselves as being able to do anything significant for God, but we are a perfect candidate to be used by Him as a blessing to someone else.

I'm so glad David was a man after God's own heart. Because if it had been me, I would have said, "All right, so you want to act like this? I brought you a sandwich, but I'm going to put it right back in my pocket since you're such a smart aleck!"

That's the difference between me and David.

How does God choose His person? He chooses based upon the heart, and He chooses the least likely. Have we ever been put down? Told we'd never amount to anything? Judged by whatever season of life we were in? We might not see ourselves, even now, as being able to do anything significant for God. But based upon God's criterion for choosing, we are a perfect candidate to be used by Him as a blessing to somebody else.

God chooses the least likely people. Technically and culturally, the older brothers should have been the most favored. But God said He was looking for someone different. We need to be careful that our traditions don't get in the way of a fresh wind of God.

He doesn't promise that we won't go through stuff. He just promises that we won't have to go through it alone.

Israel was one of the few nations during that time that inaugurated people for office through the anointing of oil. The oil symbolized a contract. So when someone was anointed, God obligated himself to that person. It was as if He said, "I'm in this thing with you."

Deliverance Through the Fire

On the day of Pentecost, after Christ ascended, He sent the Holy Spirit to live inside of us permanently. There's nothing we can do to make the Holy Spirit leave us. He who indwells us says, "I will never leave you or forsake you," and "Lo, I am with you even to the ends of the earth."

If we have given our life to Jesus Christ, then we are indwelt with the person and the power of the Holy Spirit, and God has obligated Himself to us. We are in a contractual relationship, which means we will never have to face a battle or a trial by ourselves. He doesn't promise that we won't go through stuff. He just promises that we won't have to go through it alone.

Remember how Shadrach, Meshach and Abednego defied the king? (Daniel 3:1-23). The king said, "If you don't bow down I'm going to put you into the fire."

Daniel said, "Look, King Nebuchadnezzar, we will not bow down to you. Our God can and will deliver us from the fire. But if not, I'm still not going to bow down to you." Note that the phrase "but if not" is important.

We might think deliverance from God would mean deliverance from the fire. But it means deliverance through the fire.

The king roared, "Heat up that furnace to seven times its usual temperature!"

So his servants made the fire so fierce that it burned them up.

We might think deliverance from God would mean deliverance from the fire. But it doesn't. It means deliverance *through* the fire. God allowed the young men to get into the fire. But when Nebuchadnezzar looked into the furnace he said, "I know we threw three people in there but I see four people walking through the fire, and one of them looks like the Son of God!"

Friends, God has obligated himself to us, not to keep us out of the fire but to get into the fire with us, so while we're walking in it we won't be hurt. He will deliver us through the fire because there's a covenant contract on our life.

In the next chapter we'll learn new things about David—especially about his missed opportunities in engaging with his family. God chose David because of the humility He saw in David's heart. God stayed with him during his trials and mistakes because He obligated Himself to deliver David through the fire.

As we will discover, David's humility propelled him to the palace, but God's anointing delivered him through the fire of his mistakes.

WORKBOOK

Chapter 1 Questions

Question: In our text, God chose the least likely person to be named king. Describe a time in your life when God chose you or someone else for a difficult task. What was your reaction?

_____
_____
_____
_____
_____
_____
_____
_____
_____
_____
_____
_____

Question: Samuel was given the task of choosing the next king. He wanted to choose from the men who had the right appearance. In what ways have you been tempted to choose using your own criteria instead of God's? How will you begin to redirect your actions toward submitting to God?

_____
_____
_____
_____
_____
_____
_____
_____
_____
_____
_____

Question: The person we think little of may be the person God has chosen to do great things. In what ways have you hindered God's plan for your life, your child, or someone around you because you didn't see what God was doing?

_____
_____
_____
_____
_____

Question: Are you aware of God's calling for you? If so, what is it and how will you respond? If not, what will you do to seek His will for your current situation? What fears are holding you back?

Question: Our important relationships define who we are. Sometimes people are unknowingly holding us back from doing what God has for us. How do you need to change your relationships so God can move? What will you do to move in the way God has planned for you and not according to how others perceive you?

_____

_____

_____

_____

_____

_____

_____

_____

_____

_____

Action: When God tells us to go somewhere, we had better get over our fear and go. Submit yourself in humility to what God wants for you. Remember that what God is going to do in your life He's been setting up since before you were born—in fact, even before your parents and grandparents were born. Don't ever think that your being here is an accident. God has a perfect plan for your life.

Chapter 1 Notes

CHAPTER TWO

Missed Opportunities of Fatherhood

We've seen that David was a man after God's own heart, the anointed one of Yahweh. The story of David so far has led us from the sheepfold to Goliath, then from Goliath to the palace.

As we continue reading about the life of David, our focus shifts in a totally different direction. We will see David's family beginning to be destabilized and his kingdom unraveling because of his serious mistakes. But more importantly, we will see how we can learn from those mistakes today.

We begin with 2 Samuel 13:1.

> *David's son Absalom had a beautiful sister named Tamar, and David's son Amnon was infatuated with her. Amnon was frustrated to the point of making himself sick over his sister Tamar, because she was a virgin, but it seemed impossible to do anything to her.*

> Amnon had a friend named Jonadab, a son of David's brother Shimeah. Jonadab was a very shrewd man, and he asked Amnon, "Why are you, the king's son, so miserable every morning? Won't you tell me?"
>
> Amnon replied, "I'm in love with Tamar, my brother Absalom's sister." Jonadab said to him, "Lie down on your bed and pretend you're sick. When your father comes to see you, say to him, "Please let my sister Tamar come and give me something to eat. Let her prepare food in my presence so I can watch and eat it from her hand."
>
> So Amnon lay down and pretended to be sick. When the king came to see him, Amnon said to him, "Please let my sister Tamar come and make a couple of cakes in my presence so I can eat from her hand."
>
> David sent word to Tamar at the palace: "Please go to your brother Amnon's house and prepare a meal for him." Then Tamar went to his house while Amnon was lying down. She took dough, kneaded it, made cakes in his presence, and baked them.
>
> She brought the pan and set it down in front of him, but he refused to eat. Amnon said, "Everyone leave me!" And everyone left him. "Bring the meal to the bedroom," Amnon told Tamar, "so I can eat from your hand." Tamar took the cakes she had made and went to her brother Amnon's bedroom.
>
> When she brought them to him to eat, he grabbed her and said, "Come, sleep with me, my sister!" "Don't, my brother!" she cried. "Don't humiliate me, for such a thing should never be done in Israel. Don't do this horrible thing! Where could I ever go with my disgrace? And you— you would be like one of the immoral men in Israel! — **2 Samuel 13:1-13**

Tamar was saying, "Don't do this to me. If you do, where would I be able to hold up my head again? And you would look like a fool to everyone. This is outrageous. You'll bring shame on me.

Now watch how she tries to get out of it.

Please, speak to the king, for he won't keep me from you." But he refused to listen to her, and because he was stronger than she was, he raped her.

After this, Amnon hated Tamar with such intensity that the hatred he hated her with was greater than the love he had loved her with. "Get out of here!" he said.

"No," she cried, "sending me away is much worse than the great wrong you've already done to me!" But he refused to listen to her. Instead, he called to the servant who waited on him: "Throw this woman out and bolt the door behind her!" Amnon's servant threw her out and bolted the door behind her. Now Tamar was wearing a long-sleeved garment, because this is what the king's virgin daughters wore. Tamar put ashes on her head and tore the long-sleeved garment she was wearing. She put her hand on her head and went away crying out.

Her brother Absalom said to her: "Has your brother Amnon been with you? Be quiet for now, my sister. He is your brother. Don't take this thing to heart." So Tamar lived as a desolate woman in the house of her brother Absalom.

When King David heard about all these things, he was furious. Absalom didn't say anything to Amnon, either good or bad, because he hated Amnon since he disgraced his sister Tamar. — **2 Samuel 13:13-22**

The story of David and Absalom is the closing phase of the Davidic biography. Meanwhile, we have seen an ugly side of David. You may have read the story of Bathsheba, and David's acts of adultery and murder that took place with Uriah and Bathsheba. (This is recorded in 2 Samuel 11 and 12). Now more ugly aspects of the great king are about to be exposed. But one thing we must be careful to remember is that David was still what

God declared him to be from the start. He was still a man after God's own heart, and God was still with him through the fire.

Although David's mistakes had consequences, God never took His hand off of his life.

Before David ever messed up, God said He was looking for a man after His own heart, someone who would be better than his neighbor. He found that person in the sheepfold, and despite his subsequent failures, he was still who God declared him to be.

Although David's mistakes had consequences, God never took His hand off of his life. The consequences of David's mistakes affected his children in ways he could never have imagined. But God was still in control.

An Imperfect Family Tree

Let us look first at David's family relationships. Amnon, the one who raped Tamar, was David's firstborn son, and would have been the logical heir to his throne. Absalom was David's third son. (He had a second son by Abigail, whose name was Chileab, but we only hear about him once in all of Scripture.)

Some scholars have argued that this thing between Absalom and Amnon was really a power play for the throne. I have a hard time believing that, because

Absalom was third in line for the throne and to get it, he would have had to take out both Amnon and Chileab.

But what he was calling "love" was really an unhealthy and destructive lust.

Tamar, daughter of David, was Absalom's full sister and Amnon's half-sister. Jonadab, the man who gave Amnon all that "great advice" was David's nephew and Amnon's cousin. Apparently Tamar's beauty caused her brother Amnon to lose his mind over her. The text says he was pretty much sick with love.

His cousin came in and said, "Oh my king, why are you moaning every single morning and acting like something is wrong?" But what Amnon was calling "love" was really an unhealthy and destructive lust. He said, "I love my sister Tamar" but it was a lie. He was self-deceived.

Verse 14 says, "But he refused to listen to her, and because he was stronger than she was, he raped her."

> After this, Amnon hated Tamar with such intensity that the hatred he hated her with was greater than the love he had loved her with. "Get out of here!" he said. — *2 Samuel 13:15*

This was important because in Israel, the law required that a man who had sexual intercourse with a virgin had to marry her, according to Exodus 22:16-17:

> *If a man seduces a virgin who is not engaged, and he has sexual relations with her, he must certainly pay the bride-price for her to be his wife. If her father absolutely refuses to give her to him, he must pay an amount in silver equal to the bridal price for virgins.* — **Exodus 22:16-17**

You couldn't just take a woman's virginity at no cost or commitment. This is why sexuality in today's western culture is so cheap. A woman often gives up for free what is very valuable. But it doesn't matter how costly your possession is if you don't put a premium on it yourself. So many women don't realize this, partly because they've grown up without fathers putting into their spirit just how valuable they are. So they allow guys to get up into their heads. Having placed no value on themselves, they allow this stuff in their ear to define them.

The text says that after they had sex, Amnon hated Tamar with the same passion that he had "loved" her with. What do you do when the person you've given your body to turns around and dogs you out later? What do you do when the initial act of sex was never from a place of love but from a place of lust and eventually hatred? Most of the time a woman is coming from a place of love, while the man is just coming from a place of lust. That's why it's so jacked up from the beginning. We can never trust a love whose starting point takes us outside of God's order.

In Revelation 2, the Ephesian church had left their first love for idol worship. Some of us may have left our first love for a man or woman. A so-called "love" that leads us down a path of leaving our first love is not a love to be trusted and is something we are to run from. If we find that because of his or her "love" we are drifting further away from what we know is God's standard and ideal, that is not a love that is going to be healthy for us.

Let's be careful we don't allow our relationships to get in the middle of what God wants to do in our life.

We may be dating somebody and find our attendance at the weekly Bible study is now down to once a month. Now that we're dating so-and-so, we don't spend as much time in our devotional. We don't spend time in the Bible because every time we try, the text messages start arriving. (We shouldn't even have the phone next to us when we're in the Word!). Let's be careful we don't allow our relationships to get in the middle of what God wants to do in our life.

Let's return to our text. Look at verse 16 and notice the first cultural point. If you slept with a virgin, you were supposed to pay the bride-price and marry her.

> "No!" she cried, "sending me away is much worse than the great wrong you've already done to me!" But he refused to listen to her. — *2 Samuel 13:16*

Here's why: The term translated "sending away" is the term for *divorce*.

> *If a man marries a woman, but she becomes displeasing to him because he finds something improper about her, he may write her a divorce certificate, hand it to her, and send her away from his house.* — **Deuteronomy 24:1**

So being sent away is the same as being divorced. Tamar is saying that Amnon would only be compounding the problem. She says, "You've raped me. You will not do the right thing by marrying me. Yet you act as if we have been married by sending me out as though I had done something to displease you."

> *Instead, he called to the servant who waited on him: "Throw this woman out and bolt the door behind her! Amnon's servant threw her out and bolted the door behind her. Now Tamar was wearing a long-sleeved garment, because this is what the king's virgin daughters wore.* — **2 Samuel 13:17-18**

When she tore her robe, after being kicked out, it signified that her life was ruined, for she was no longer what she used to be.

So often I see my dear sisters with symbolic torn robes. I see it in their faces, in their emotions, and in their actions. Some of you were never raped physically but you were raped emotionally, and you wear the look of a ruined life all over your face, the look that says you are no longer who you used to be. But I've got news for you: The God you have come to serve has a new robe and a new set of clothes for you. In Christ your identity no longer has to be shaped by the hurt or the shame or the pain of your past.

We always want to focus on fixing the situation but we seldom focus on healing the person.

You can be healed and restored today if you will just surrender yourself to the Lord and all that He has for you. I hear the Lord saying, "Today you can be healed, and I've got new clothes for you! You can be restored to the stately person I designed you to be."

In this section, I want to point out some opportunities David missed as a father. But I will also point out opportunities for fathers today, and for parents at large.

Look again at verses 19 and 20,

> Tamar put ashes on her head and tore the long-sleeved garment she was wearing. She put her hand on her head and went away crying out. — *2 Samuel 13:19*
>
> Her brother Absalom said to her: "Has your brother Amnon been with you? Be quiet for now, my sister. He is your brother. Don't take this thing to heart." So Tamar lived as a desolate woman in the house of her brother Absalom. — *2 Samuel 13:20*

The text says that Tamar moved in with Absalom her brother. Don't miss the advice he gave her: "Hold your peace!" In other words, "Tamar I want you to live in silence and keep your pain to yourself."

This is built into the DNA of men. We always want to focus on fixing the situation but we seldom focus on healing the person. We think that if we can make more money, or buy a new house, or buy a car for her, all will be well. And we get frustrated as men when we've done all that we thought we could do to make her happy and she's still not happy.

The cohabitation of pain and anger creates a dysfunctional atmosphere.

For most of us, it is easier to fix problems then to heal wounds. And the rest of 2 Samuel is about people trying to solve problems but never truly dealing with the wounds of the hurt people involved.

We have Tamar who is in pain, living with Absalom who is furious. We have pain and anger cohabitating with each other. And nothing good will ever come out of that situation. I've seen this over the years as I've counseled couples. You have a sister who is in pain over life and a brother who is angry with life. The cohabitation of pain and anger creates a dysfunctional atmosphere. And when you add children to the mix, you're bringing them into an already unhealthy situation, continuing the dysfunction to the next generation.

So Tamar moves in with Absalom, and now we have pain and anger cohabitating, making for a bad atmosphere in the house. Then David, as a father and a king, compounds these problems through his lack of action.

When you have God's authority on your life to correct and to bring order, you cannot be passive.

Missed Opportunity One: Lack of Action

Look at verse 21: *When King David heard about all these things, he was furious (2 Samuel 13:21 HCSB).* Notice that the verse stops there because David stopped there. The first missed opportunity for David as a father was his inaction. His daughter had been raped by one of his sons, and all he could do was muster up emotion but no action. So now we have David who was angry and Absalom who was angry. One would not act, and the other would act in an inappropriate manner—all because the first one did nothing.

David was God's anointed, his appointed authority. And when you have God's authority on your life to correct and to bring order, you cannot be passive, because the enemy will come in to fill the vacuum. Men, do you want to see the enemy run amuck in your family? Do you want to see chaos in your family? The enemy will get a foothold in that mess and create havoc.

When you have authority on your life, inactivity is unacceptable. Fathers, God placed the mantle of leadership on your life for a reason. He gave it to you so you could take dominion here in the earthly realm. Don't you know that the greatest victory over the enemy has already been won on the cross of Jesus Christ?

Most of the stuff that happens in our lives is not necessarily because we've done something wrong but because we've done nothing at all.

And that same authority has been given to you! He's given you the keys to the kingdom so whatever you bind on earth shall be bound in heaven, and whatever you release on earth shall be released in heaven. The victory is already yours if you will step into that authority and use it.

Most of the stuff that happens in our lives is not necessarily because we've done something wrong but because we've done nothing at all. In this story, all David could do was stew in his anger. This represents the psychological DNA of many men. Most men are thinkers, with an array of private thoughts. We ponder things and we think them through.

Sister, if you ever want to get lost in a crazy world, get lost in the crazy world of your man's thoughts. Allow yourself to spend half a day there. The private world of a man is the land of the lost, and I speak from personal experience. We are daydreamers. We will sit in an office and daydream of having our boss's office, but most of the time we won't do anything about it.

We have a lot of dreams, but seldom do we muster up the required courage and self-discipline to make them a reality.

Our private thoughts are many. Most men can envision a better life for their family and their home and most men will re-imagine their future and the generations that will flow from them. I don't know of any Christian brother who dreams of generations of dysfunction, but many brothers cannot translate those private thoughts into actionable items that will move the needle forward in their family or situation. We have a lot of dreams, but seldom do we muster up the required courage and self-discipline to make them a reality.

I see David here at the point of paralysis. I see him with all these thoughts and emotions, all this anger, and yet he takes no action. Why? Here was a man who had stepped up to Goliath and had dealt with Saul. Here was a man who was about to take Nabal out, a man who defeated the armies of the Philistines. Why didn't he take action in his own family?

Could it be that his own guilt prevented him from confronting Amnon and addressing the pain of Tamar?

Earlier in the book of 2 Samuel, we can read how David had slept with Bathsheba. Then he had his colleague murdered. Even before the murder, he tried to get Uriah drunk, hoping he would go and sleep with Bathsheba and think Bathsheba's baby was his.

Do you see the mess here? The apple doesn't fall too far from the tree. Both David and Amnon had been driven by lust and had to get their woman by any means necessary: David by deception and murder and Amnon by rape. David had to have Bathsheba and would kill to get her. Amnon had to have Tamar and would rape to get her. Both men were cut from the same cloth. Here was David's firstborn, following the pattern of his father.

Guilt is a funny thing. It will play mind games and tricks on us.

I can almost imagine David cowering in fear. *How can I deal with this when I've had such a mess in my own life and everybody knows about the dirt I've done? How can I chastise Amnon in the light of my own sins?*

Guilt is a funny thing. It will play mind games and tricks on us. I can relate to David. And without giving up too much because I want to respect my son's privacy, I can see so much of myself in my son at this stage of the game. So I struggle. How do I approach him?

I see someone who loves money and the high life. So instead of going to school full-time, he gets a job. Why? So he can have a nice car. Why? So he can impress the girls. I see that. And by the way, I'm not just talking about my son. I'm talking about me. I played around in school, went to college, and treated it like a high school. I messed around so I could get a good job working at Aerospace Cooperation with my mother.

So at eighteen, I and my friend KJ, my current sound engineer, were working for the Aerospace Cooperation and I was making $320 a week. Back in 1986 that was a lot of money, and I was still on my mama's insurance. So every dime I made was all mine. I was flossing a Nissan 200 SX. Black on black, the kind where the lights would go up. I was rolling down a busy street with my lights on in the middle of the day and the radio booming, all to impress. And when you get a car, your expenses go up so you have to work longer hours to keep up the lifestyle you started.

Don't you just love the grace of God? When your life should have gone in one direction, grace stepped in.

In other words, delayed gratification is not in the Moore family DNA. At twenty-two years I went off to start college. Everyone else had graduated while I was still messing around and sleeping around. Stuff that was outside of God's order for my life. In 2013, I was seeing the same template manifest in my son—who has since found his way back to reflecting God's heart. But at the time, I worried how I could guide him when he knew my own story.

I faced a really big problem. Not only did he see my story, but he also saw the grace on my life. So he could say, "Dad, you did all that and now look at you! You're a successful pastor of a church. You've been married for almost fifteen years. You got a graduate degree and you're respected in the community. So why can't I live my life and still pull it off?"

I could see I would have a better testimony if I were divorced and living under a bridge. It might have worked better, I mused, if I could say to my son, "See what happens when you go down that path? Look at me!" But that's not my story.

We cannot let the enemy use our guilt to prevent us from standing in our current assignment.

Don't you just love the grace of God? When your life should have gone in one direction, grace stepped in.

God says, "Yes, you should be under a bridge. Yes, you should be destitute. Yes, you should have a broken marriage. But I'm going to put my grace on you so you can stand and enjoy fifteen years of marriage, a church that is thriving, and respect in the community. And by the way, Jody, you don't deserve any of it. It's because of My grace and favor on your life."

But that didn't solve my problem. How would I tell my son he was messing up and heading in the wrong direction? So I understand David's predicament.

However, we cannot let the enemy use our guilt to prevent us from standing in our current assignment. Yes, stuff happened back then, but we've got an assignment today.

We can never allow our past mistakes to tether us. I did that stuff back in 1986, but in 2013 my son needed the Jody of 2013. If we have children, we owe it to them to stand in the authority we have in Christ and deal with that mess in our house. Let's not allow the enemy to use our past to dilute the power and the potency of our future.

I think David got stuck. *How can I address this in him when I know all the stuff I've done?*

Look at verse 22.

> *Absalom didn't say anything to Amnon, either good or bad, because he hated Amnon since he disgraced his sister Tamar.* — 2 Samuel 13:22

Absalom has told Tamar to remain silent to nurse her wounded heart. He chooses to keep silent to fuel his raging anger. David is angry but will not say anything. The bottom line here is, nobody's talking. We have one wounded woman, two angry men, and another man who is abusive. So much pain and disappointment and yet nobody's saying anything. And this went on for two years!

Missed Opportunity Two: Lack of Engagement

We have now our second missed opportunity for David. The first was his lack of action. The second one was a lack of engagement. David never reached out to Absalom to meet his son where he was, to guide him through his emotions of anger and betrayal. Absalom's anger only grew and became more intense over that two year period.

What was happening with David happens to many men. We wait too long to engage. And we expect them to come to us. Or when we finally do engage it's because something has made disengagement no longer an option. So instead of engaging from a healthy place, we engage from a reactionary place.

> Then [Absalom] went to the king and said, "Your servant has just hired sheepshearers. Will the king and his servants please come with your servant?"
>
> The king replied to Absalom, "No, my son, we should not all go, or we would be a burden to you." Although Absalom urged him, he wasn't willing to go, though he did bless him.
>
> "If not," Absalom said, "please let my brother Amnon go with us."
>
> The king asked him, "Why should he go with you?" — **2 Samuel 13:24-26**

It seems David was suspicious that something was up. David knew of the anger and bitterness between his sons, but he never acted on his gut instinct. And herein lies another difference between men and women. Women will often act on their gut instinct while men often second guess themselves. And it's in second guessing himself that David has set his family up for destruction.

> *Now Absalom commanded his young men, "Watch Amnon until he is in a good mood from the wine. When I order you to strike Amnon, then kill him. Don't be afraid. Am I not the one who has commanded you? Be strong and courageous! So Absalom's young men did to Amnon just as Absalom had commanded. Then all the rest of the king's sons got up, and each fled on his mule.* — **2 Samuel 13:28-29**

So inaction and a lack of engagement from David led to destructive behavior in his son.

Some adults are walking around today with wounds that were never healed from childhood. So they make dysfunctional decisions that could have been avoided if their parents had dealt with some issues earlier.

Parents, your inaction, and lack of engagement will cause emotions that are right now hidden and buried to spring up later in ways that will take people out. If you don't step up in the authority that is yours, you will lose an opportunity down the line to deal with stuff that could have been dealt with at the early stages of your child's life.

I believe there are some adults walking around today with wounds that were never healed from childhood. So they make dysfunctional decisions that could have been avoided if their parents had dealt with some issues earlier.

In the text there is some tension that I wrestle with, and it may be a tension for others as well. How could

David really have stepped in when everybody in the situation was an adult? Amnon had grown, Absalom had grown, and Tamar had grown. But the fact that David was the king meant that each of his children lived off him. They had what they had because their house was royal property. Their food was royal and their clothes were royal.

My point is this: I don't care how adult your child is, if they live under your roof then you've got something to say about it. If they are eating your food, wearing clothes you've paid for, going to the hospital off your insurance, you have the right to set the rules—even if they have their own job and car.

As soon as you abdicate your parental responsibility in the name of your kids being grown up, you circumvent what God is trying to do.

You need to step up in your authority and say, "As long as you are under this roof I have a right to speak. Your behavior is out of line. When you are too grown to hear what I have to say, get your stuff, get your clothes, empty your closet, walk out that door, buy your own food, pay your own rent, pay your own insurance and do whatever you want to do. But as long as you are in my house you are going to listen to what I have to say.

Take authority over that mess. Did you ever think that maybe God has sovereignly kept them in your house because there's still some stuff they need to learn from you, that they were neither spiritually nor emotionally ready for? As soon as you abdicate your responsibility in the name of their being grown up, you circumvent what God is trying to do. Your children will pick up on your abdication and seek to break out from your authority. But God is not going to release them until you fulfill your assignment in their life.

David could have avoided so much pain if he had just spoken up and engaged with his family. I don't want to beat up David too much, however, because I understand how guilt can paralyze you. Sometimes I have to wrestle with my own personal "demons" of guilt just to talk to my own son. I've often prayed in the shower, *Lord, why did I mess up so much?*

Missed Opportunity Three: Failure to Create an Environment to Fail in Safety

David's inaction and lack of engagement played a part in Amnon being killed.

> While they were on their way, a report reached David: "Absalom struck down all the king's sons; not even one of them survived!" In response the king stood up, tore his clothes, and lay down on the ground; and all his servants stood by with their clothes torn.
>
> But Jonadab, son of David's brother Shimeah, spoke up: 'My lord must not think they have killed all the young men, the king's sons, because only Amnon is dead. In fact, Absalom has planned this ever since the day Amnon disgraced his sister Tamar. So now, my lord the king, don't take seriously the report that says

all the king's sons are dead. Only Amnon is dead." — 2 Samuel 13:30-33

From the day Tamar was raped, two years before, Absalom had been planning this event. He'd stayed cool for two years. He'd been angry, but he had so much discipline around his wrath that he just sat on it. Some have said that the essence of a terrorist is to be angry but to have the discipline to be still until the time is right. Don't you know the 9/11 terrorists planned their attacks for years before finally striking the World Trade Center?

Absalom laid low for two years, and then murdered his brother, the first in line to the throne.

Meanwhile, Absalom had fled.

When the young man who was standing watch looked up, there were many people coming from the road west of him from the side of the mountain.

Jonadab said to the king, "Look, the king's sons have come! It's exactly like your servant said."

Just as he finished speaking, the king's sons entered and wept loudly. Then the king and all his servant also wept bitterly.

Now Absalom fled and went to Talmai son of Ammihud, king of Geshur. And David mourned for his son every day.

*Absalom had fled and gone to Geshur where he stayed three years. Then King David longed to go to Absalom, for David had finished grieving over Amnon's death. — **2 Samuel 13:34-39***

The writer tells us three times in four verses that Absalom fled. And here we see David's third missed opportunity. Remember he had missed opportunities to act and to be engaged. Now he had missed an opportunity to create a safe environment for his children to fail in.

Our kids are going to make mistakes. As parents, we have a responsibility to set an atmosphere for them to fail in safety. This doesn't mean there is no accountability or consequences for poor behavior, but it does mean there is an atmosphere in the home that breeds transparency.

The enemy's breeding ground for sin and destructive living is secrecy. He loves an atmosphere where you can hide and duck. As a matter of fact, he operates best in darkness. If we live a life of secrecy, we make it a safe place for the enemy to get a foothold in our life and sow destructive seeds and destructive behaviors.

Many of us grew up without a safe place for mistakes, to this day we would rather live a double life than one that is transparent and open.

Many of us live double lives as adults because we had to live a double life growing up. As children we had no safe place for mistakes. There were always consequences but never grace and restoration. So to this day we would rather live a double life than one that is transparent and open.

So Absalom ran. Running from our mistakes seems to have been built into the DNA of man since the Fall.

Genesis 3 is a familiar passage. Adam and Eve sinned. Eve listened to the serpent, ate the fruit, gave it to her husband, and he ate it too. Then they both realized they were naked and put some leaves over themselves. Now they were fleeing through the garden. Look at verses 8-12:

> Then the man and his wife heard the sound of the LORD God walking in the garden at the time of evening breeze, and they hid themselves from the LORD God among the trees of the garden. So the LORD God called out to the man and said to him, "Where are you?"
>
> And he said, "I heard You in the garden and I was afraid because I was naked; so I hid."
>
> Then He asked, "Who told you that you were naked? Did you eat from the tree that I commanded you not to eat from?"
>
> Then the man replied, 'The woman You gave to be with me—she gave me some fruit from the tree, and I ate it." — **Genesis 3:8-12**

So they're fleeing, having made a big mistake. Let's read on from verse 20:

> Adam named his wife Eve, because she was the mother of all the living. The LORD God made clothing out of skins for Adam and his wife, and He clothed them. — **Genesis 3:20-21**

From the very beginning it has been our default response to run and hide. But it is God as a father who goes after us. Yes, he pronounced consequences and judgment. But notice how he still covered up the shame of their nakedness.

I believe God placed in the DNA of men a gift of covering. We have the God-given ability to cover our wives, but we also have the God-given ability to cover our children. It is our responsibility to set the atmosphere in our homes. And we must strive to set an atmosphere of safety along with an atmosphere of accountability.

So Absalom ran. And many of our children today are still in running mode as well. Some of us have never stopped running since childhood. We live in retreat mode when there is no hope of grace. Some of us never found the safe place to fail, and some of us as parents haven't provided a safe place to fail for our kids. But if we can just step up and take action and engage in our kid's lives, we can show them grace and reconciliation.

While they were driving to the store, he was "almost passing razor blades," thinking about what he had to do.

From Action and Engagement to Grace

Chuck Swindoll, one of my favorite preachers, was pastor of First Evangelical Free Church in Fullerton, California for almost twenty years, and now pastors in

Dallas, Texas. He tells a story from his youth when he was working at a Five and Dime. He pilfered six softballs and hid them in his room.

When his mother was putting his underwear and socks away she discovered the six softballs stuck in the back of his drawer. And of course when Daddy got home she told him what she had found. Chuck Swindoll says Daddy immediately put Chuck in the car and they drove all the way to the store because Daddy was going to make Chuck get out and confess to his boss that he'd stolen the softballs.

Chuck says that while they were driving to the store he was "almost passing razor blades," thinking about what he had to do.

When they got to the store Chuck went in while his Daddy stayed in the car, because he had to do this on his own. So Chuck went in and made his confession to the boss. Of course his boss fired him, and Chuck staggered back to the car.

Be careful not to go overboard. When you overreact, it creates a situation where the person doesn't even want to deal with you anymore.

On the way home his dad rebuilt his emotions and his confidence. He had done wrong and he had to learn an incredible lesson. But Swindoll says his father didn't overdo it. He drilled into him that when you steal, you get fired. But if you didn't lose your job you lost something even worse than that, your self-respect and your dignity.

Swindoll says there was something like an ornament of grace that came around his neck from his father. To his knowledge his father never told anyone else about it. And he never mentioned it again.

A couple of things stand out to me from Swindoll's story. First, his father didn't overdo it. Be careful, men that you do not go overboard. When you overreact, it creates a situation where the person doesn't even want to deal with you anymore. I'm not just talking about your children; I'm talking about your wife too. This principle applies in the home generally. Is somebody keeping secrets from you because you can't handle the truth? Stop making it hard for people to engage you in confession and transparency. You want folk to be able to talk to you but how can they when you go overboard every time?

Embedded in the nucleus of grace is the very power of redemption.

Some of us block ourselves off from healthy conversation. Why should I try to tell you something if you have no mastery of your own emotions?

The other thing that sticks out to me from Swindoll's story is where he says his father put around his neck an ornament of grace. Embedded in the nucleus of grace is the very power of redemption. Paul says in Ephesians 2:8, "By grace you have been saved through faith." In other words, grace always lead to redemption, and redemption is the launching pad for restoration. Grace is when God gives you what you don't deserve.

My father-in-law, Bishop Kenneth Ulmer, tells the story of when my wife Keniya was a little girl. She wanted some milk and filled a big glass with it.

"Don't drink that milk in the living room," he told her, "because if you drink that milk in the living room and spill it, you're going to get a spanking."

If justice is getting what you deserve, mercy is not getting what you deserve.

Later my father-in-law was working in his study and getting ready for Sunday when he heard crying from outside the room. He walked out and sure enough, there was glass on the floor and milk spilled all over it. He stepped up to Keniya and saw tears streaming down her face. He saw such remorse and brokenness. So instead of doing what he said he was going to do which was to spank her—and it would have been well-deserved—he found a paper towel, got down on the floor and began to clean up the mess.

Mercy is when you don't get what you deserve.

About an hour later he realized he didn't have a particular book that he needed for his preparation. So they drove to get the book, and on the way they were going past 31 Flavors. Of course she looked over at him and said, "I want ice cream."

So what did he do? His car miraculously—of its own volition—turned around and drove into 31 Flavors. And he got out and he bought her an ice cream.

If justice is getting what you deserve, mercy is *not* getting what you deserve—in this case a spanking. And grace is when you get the ice cream.

Is anybody right now living in some grace blessing? You know you should have been punished. You know where you're supposed to be, but God in his mercy said "I'm not going to give you what you deserve. In fact, I'm going to turn around clean up your mess, and give you what you *don't* deserve."

When we create a home where accountability and grace are the bookends of our response to failures, we create a home where God can do his work in the hearts of our children.

I'm so glad God is a God of grace because not only did he withhold from me what I deserved, but I'm here today because of what I didn't deserve. That's grace. We are never more like Jesus than when we are showing love and dispensing grace. When we create a home where accountability and grace are the bookends of our response to failures, we create a home where God can do his work in the hearts of our children.

Hebrews 1:3 tells us that Jesus was the exact expression of the Father. In other words, we know what the Father looks like when we look at Jesus. Well, our children know the character of their heavenly Father by watching us. So we had better be careful how we handle them.

We've seen how David failed to take action with his sons. He failed to discipline Amnon and to engage Absalom and create a safe environment for him to fail. We must never forget that God works through both discipline and grace to build up godly offspring who will bring Him glory. We would be wrong if we thought our responsibility as parents was only to make a worldly success of our children. Our discipline and our grace will set God up to do something great in their lives down the line.

We can be rough and tough when we have to be, but we need to know how to balance that with kindness, mercy, and grace.

Don't be afraid to use the rod when necessary. But brothers, don't think that it diminishes your manhood when you handle your children, especially your boys, with gentleness and kindness. The world might have taught us to be rough and tough with our boys. But God did not. We can be rough and tough when we have to be, but we need to know how to balance that with kindness, mercy, and grace.

> *Absalom fled and went to Talmai son of Ammihud, king of Geshur. And David mourned for his son every day.* — **2 Samuel 13:37**

So Absalom fled to King Talmai who was his maternal grandfather. People never run in a vacuum. When they run *from* something they run *to* something or someone. Praise God Absalom was able to find safety with his grandfather. But how many times do our children run to the wrong thing and to the wrong person? When they do, we need to ask ourselves two questions: What are they running from? And what do they see in this person, versus what they see in me, that makes them so safe to run to?

So many of us spend our time complaining about the ungodly boyfriend when we ought to be wondering what is wrong with our daughter that she would go after someone who acts like he does.

When our daughter whom we've poured so much into hooks up with an ungodly boyfriend, we need to ask ourselves, "What was she running from? And what is it about this person that she would run to?" Especially when we've taught her certain things that should make this person appear unacceptable to her. How is it that she is so empty inside, with such low self-esteem, that she would find safety with a guy who was so dysfunctional?"

So many of us men spend our time complaining about the ungodly boyfriend when we ought to be wondering what is wrong with our daughter that she would go after someone who acts like he does. Let's stop chewing out the boyfriend and instead put our eyes on our daughter or son. Why do they feel safe with this person? What were they not getting at home?

What have I missed as a father? What didn't I see? Well either I was too busy or had my head in the sand. We've said that David probably didn't engage his son over his mistake because he'd made so many mistakes himself. David's guilt prevented him from receiving authentic reconciliation, therefore, he could not convey that to his sons.

David was a man after God's own heart, but he had a difficult time dealing with and respond to his own emotions.

Missed Opportunity Four: Failure to Leverage Authentic Reconciliation

David's fourth missed opportunity of fatherhood was the failure to leverage the power of authentic reconciliation that would lead to life-changing restoration.

After Absalom fled and went to Geshur, he stayed there three years. And King David longed to go to Absalom, for he was consoled concerning Amnon's death. — **2 Samuel 13:38-39 (NIV)**

Remember, David was a man after God's own heart. He was still the greatest king who ever lived. This had not changed. But David was a man who had a difficult time dealing with and responding to his own emotions. He was angry and didn't deal with it. He longed for his son and didn't do anything about it. He did not respond well to his own anger and grief. He had a son whom he longed to reach out to but couldn't. And as long as he would not reach out, his son would stay distant.

The one who has the authority should be the one reaching out in reconciliation.

In any relationship where reconciliation and restoration is the agenda somebody has to make the first move, and it should always be the stronger one. In other words, the one who has the authority should be the one reaching out. David wasn't just the king. More importantly he was the father and the stronger of the two. He should have been the one reaching out to and engaging his son.

Fathers, you are the one in authority. You are the providers. You should be the ones reaching out to your wife and children. Let me give you a hint of how it works in the Moore house when I have to discipline my children. If I have punished them in a way that makes them feel really bad, I will send them to their room. I will give them a break of maybe thirty minutes, but I will always make my way to their room, wrap my arms around them and let them know it's okay.

"Daddy was upset, but it's over with now. I love you. You messed up, but we are going to get through it."

I don't wait for my six-year-old daughter, or nine-year-old daughter or eleven-year-old daughter to come to me. I will not wait for my twenty-one-year-old son to come to me. I will go to them because I am still the authority figure. I am still the stronger of the two in the relationship.

And brothers, the same principle applies to your wife. The Bible says the wife is the weaker vessel. You should be the one apologizing.

Come off your high horse and learn how to use what God has placed in you to create peace in your house.

Perhaps you're saying, "But pastor, it's her fault!"

Well, get over it. Go in there and make the first move. The onus is on you to reach out for reconciliation. Lower your pride and go in there and bring her next to you. I don't care how crazy she's been.

"But pastor, she acts crazy. She's got a Jezebel spirit. She acts like a witch."

Well buddy, move that broom to the side and go on in there and love on her. Apologize.

Brothers, come off your high horse and learn how to use what God has placed in you to create peace in your house. You are the authority figure and ultimately the peacemaker. Your goal as the peacemaker is to release the power of authentic reconciliation and restore your family. If David would have stepped up as the leader and engaged with Absalom, things would likely have gone differently.

I'm so glad God reached out to me when I was stuck on stupid. I'm so glad it was God who came to me. The Bible says I love Him because He first loved me (1 John 4:19). God reaches out to us to offer us that grace because He engages us.

In the next chapter, we will be exploring what authentic reconciliation looks like in action. It goes beyond the leader or authority figure stepping up—it is a lifestyle that first begins in humility. Remember that to be people after God's own heart, we must obey God, actively engage with our families, and have a heart for authentic reconciliation.

WORKBOOK

Chapter 2 Questions

Question: For most of us, it is easier to fix problems then to heal wounds. How have you been tempted to ignore a problem or run from it to avoid the process of healing? What's keeping you from looking for healing for yourself or a family member?

_____
_____
_____
_____
_____
_____
_____
_____
_____
_____
_____

Question: Most of the stuff that happens in our lives is not necessarily because we've done something wrong but because we've done nothing at all. How has a lack of action on your part created additional problems? What can you do now to correct this?

_____
_____
_____
_____
_____
_____
_____
_____
_____
_____

Question: In which areas of your life do you have the responsibility of being the authority or a leader? How will you step up and exercise your authority and engage in your family, career, or church? What will you do differently?

_____
_____
_____
_____
_____
_____

Question: How will you reach out to a family member who made a mistake or is hurting? How will you provide a safe environment to fail and learn for those around you?

Question: God calls us to step up and reach out to our family and friends. What will you do to offer peace to someone who needs to forgive you? How will you offer your forgiveness to someone who has hurt you?

Action: Although his mistakes had consequences and guilt, God never took His hand off of David's life. Don't allow your past mistakes to tether you—especially if it pulls you away from God or loved ones. Instead, strive to establish an atmosphere of safety as well as an atmosphere of accountability. Learn how to use what God has placed in you to create peace in your house. Step out and make that first move to seek reconciliation.

Chapter 2 Notes

CHAPTER THREE

The Power of Authentic Reconciliation

God is a God of reconciliation, and you are a believer today not because you made a decision on your own. The fact is, God extended His grace to your life so you could make that decision. The Bible says we were dead in our sin, so separated from God that even our righteousness was like filthy rags (Isaiah 64:6). When we couldn't see our way through the darkness it was love that reached out and lifted us up. God intervened by acting and engaging which brought grace into our lives.

In the last chapter, we saw David wanting to go after his son but doing nothing to respond to the longing in his heart. David, who was the authority figure, should have been the one reaching out to Absalom, instead of waiting for Absalom himself or David's general Joab to take the initiative.

Joab wanted to bring Absalom home. He saw the anguish in King David's heart, so he tricked him through a woman. Doesn't this sound familiar? It's the same kind of scheme that Nathan orchestrated with David over Bathsheba. He sent a woman from Tekoa to confront David with a story:

> *Joab son of Zeruiah knew that the king's heart longed for Absalom. So Joab sent someone to Tekoa and had a wise woman brought from there. He said to her, "Pretend you are in mourning. Dress in mourning clothes, and don't use any cosmetic lotions. Act like a woman who has spent many days grieving for the dead. Then go to the king and speak these words to him." And Joab put the words in her mouth.*
>
> *When the woman from Tekoa went to the king, she fell with her face to the ground to pay him honor, and she said, "Help me, Your Majesty!"*
>
> *The king asked her, "What is troubling you?"*
>
> *She said, "I am a widow; my husband is dead. I your servant had two sons. They got into a fight with each other in the field, and no one was there to separate them. One struck the other and killed him. Now the whole clan has risen up against your servant; they say, 'Hand over the one who struck his brother down, so that we may put him to death for the life of his brother whom he killed; then we will get rid of the heir as well.' They would put out the only burning coal I have left, leaving my husband neither name nor descendant on the face of the earth."*
>
> *The king said to the woman, "Go home, and I will issue an order in your behalf."*
>
> *But the woman from Tekoa said to him, "Let my lord the king pardon me and my family, and let the king and his throne be without guilt."*
>
> *The king replied, "If anyone says anything to you, bring them to me, and they will not bother you again."*

> She said, "Then let the king invoke the LORD his God to prevent the avenger of blood from adding to the destruction, so that my son will not be destroyed."
>
> "As surely as the LORD lives," he said, "not one hair of your son's head will fall to the ground."
>
> Then the woman said, "Let your servant speak a word to my lord the king."
>
> "Speak," he replied.
>
> The woman said, "Why then have you devised a thing like this against the people of God? When the king says this, does he not convict himself, for the king has not brought back his banished son? Like water spilled on the ground, which cannot be recovered, so we must die. But that is not what God desires; rather, he devises ways so that a banished person does not remain banished from him.
>
> "And now I have come to say this to my lord the king because the people have made me afraid. Your servant thought, 'I will speak to the king; perhaps he will grant his servant's request. Perhaps the king will agree to deliver his servant from the hand of the man who is trying to cut off both me and my son from God's inheritance.'
>
> "And now your servant says, 'May the word of my lord the king secure my inheritance, for my lord the king is like an angel of God in discerning good and evil. May the Lord your God be with you.'" — *2 Samuel 14:1-17 (NIV)*

David would not have known this woman or her story. The woman was to spin this tale about two sons, one dying in a field, all to confront David with the reality of his own son whom he'd left dangling out there.

> The king said to Joab, "Very well, I will do it. Go, bring back the young man Absalom."

> *Joab fell with his face to the ground to pay him honor, and he blessed the king. Joab said, "Today your servant knows that he has found favor in your eyes, my lord the king, because the king has granted his servant's request."*
>
> *Then Joab went to Geshur and brought Absalom back to Jerusalem. But the king said, "He must go to his own house; he must not see my face." So Absalom went to his own house and did not see the face of the king.*
>
> *In all Israel there was not a man so highly praised for his handsome appearance as Absalom. From the top of his head to the sole of his foot there was no blemish in him. Whenever he cut the hair of his head—he used to cut his hair once a year because it became too heavy for him—he would weigh it, and its weight was two hundred shekels[b] by the royal standard.*
>
> *Three sons and a daughter were born to Absalom. His daughter's name was Tamar, and she became a beautiful woman.* — **2 Samuel 14:21-27 (NIV)**

It is clear that David made a half-hearted effort at reconciliation when he agreed to have Joab bring back Absalom. But he made zero effort to restore the relationship. This is the crux of the story. If David, who was the authority figure, handled this situation correctly, it would bring healing to his family. But if he handled it poorly, it would bring further destruction.

Reconciliation Starts with a Choice to Act in Humility

As husbands, wives, and parents, we need to be able to discern pivotal situations that could reshape the landscape of our family. But because we as believers, especially men, are not walking at a level of prayerful and biblical discernment—true humility—we miss major opportunities to shape the destinies of our children and our families as a whole. We are losing our children and we are losing our families.

Too many of us are missing opportunities, not just because of a lack of discernment but also because we're simply not paying attention.

The enemy has done a great job of spinning a web of deceit through the Internet and social media. Remember the good old Nickelodeon? Now we can't even watch the Disney channel. The enemy has done such a great job of distorting the minds of our children. We had better be on our game. Parenting today is not like parenting in the 70s and the 80s. And if we're not up to the challenge we're going to lose our children.

Here is an opportunity to do something that will bless the next generation. Too many of us are missing opportunities, not just because of a lack of discernment but also because we're simply not paying attention. It's hard to pay attention to our children when we're glued to *Scandal*, or busy in the TV or playing fantasy football or play station.

In David's hurt and anger, he wasn't able to deal with his son. He was unable to seek God in humility.

David may have missed the opportunity to leverage the power of authentic reconciliation, but that doesn't mean we have to make the same error. We have a choice to act or not to act..

In David's hurt and anger, he wasn't able to deal with his son. He was unable to seek God in humility to admit his emotions, and he failed to act and engage his family. This created the effect of pushing his son away. We see this in the following passage:

> The king said, 'He must go to his own house; he must not see my face.' So Absalom went to his own house and did not see the face of the king. ... Absalom lived two years in Jerusalem without seeing the king's face. — *2 Samuel 14:24, 28 (NIV)*

The key concept in this passage is presence. It is the Hebrew word *pána*, which literally means "face." We read that Absalom did not see the *face* of the king.

They hid themselves from the presence of the Lord because they were afraid.

The word *pána* is first used in Scripture in Genesis 3, after Adam and Eve sinned. They were running around, and when they realized they were naked, they covered themselves with fig leaves. The text says they hid themselves from the presence (or face) of the Lord because they were afraid.

So when David said Absalom was not to come into his presence, for the most part he was saying he needed to stay out of his face.

As I was thinking about this, I was reminded of my childhood, growing up when I lived next to a sweet old churchgoing woman whom I called Miss Ola.

I would hear her praying out of her window because I sometimes played in the alley between the houses. Unfortunately, she had a son who played minor league baseball and had got into drugs. When he came home they really struggled with his addiction to crack cocaine.

I'll never forget the time when I was around seven or eight. I was playing between the houses as usual and didn't hear this sweet lady praying as I normally did. Instead I heard her having it out with her son.

"You'd better get your blank-blank out of my face," she was saying. She was just cussing. And I can hear David saying something similar: "I don't want to see this blank-blank in my house. Keep him out of my face!"

Reconciliation means to right a relational wrong, to make peace between two parties.

In other words, "I do not want to be around him."

In Genesis Adam and Eve hid themselves from God's face to avoid being confronted with their sin. Here, in 2 Samuel chapter 14, David kept Absalom away from his face to avoid having to deal with his son and his mess. In other words, what looked like anger on the surface was really David continuing to avoid the situation with his son. He was about to miss an opportunity to use the power that we have as husbands, fathers, and parents— that is the power to right wrongs through reconciliation and restoration.

What Is True Reconciliation?

I want to show you this power we neglect sometimes in our own families. Reconciliation means to right a relational wrong, to make peace between two parties.

> *So from now on we regard no one from a worldly point of view. Though we once regarded Christ in this way, we do so no longer. Therefore, if anyone is in Christ, the new creation has come; the old has gone, the new is here! All this is from God, who reconciled us to himself through Christ and gave us the ministry of reconciliation: that God was reconciling the world to himself in Christ, not counting people's sins against them. And he has committed to us the message of reconciliation. We are therefore Christ's ambassadors, as though God were making his appeal through us. We implore you on Christ's behalf: Be reconciled to God. — 2 Corinthians 5:16-20 (NIV)*

Watch what's happening here. Paul argues that our being in Christ makes us new persons, new creations. In other words, because we are in Christ we are no longer what we used to be. The old is gone and the new has come.

Don't you know that God is done with your mess?

I love that. Paul's point is that before Christ there was an old person and an old situation. Paul is using what we call "demarcation" language. Demarcation means drawing a line in the sand. This is who we were then. And this is who we are now.

We messed up then, but we are in a better situation now. In verse 18 Paul tells us that God, through Christ reconciled us to himself and gave us the ministry of reconciliation that is in Christ. God was reconciling the world to himself, not tripping off what we did wrong. Don't you know that God is done with your stuff? He's done with your mess. The devil, who is the accuser of the saints, will often try to remind you of all the crazy stuff you used to do, but God has dealt with it. When he looks at the ledger, what you did has been wiped off. The debt has been paid, and your credit score is better than it used to be.

The Father was reaching out to a rebellious and wayward people, to folks stuck on stupid, to an adulterous generation. The Father was reaching out to reconcile us back to himself.

Real, authentic reconciliation does not happen by accident. Somebody has to step up to the plate and make it happen.

The word *reconcile* means to reestablish friendly relationships after a disagreement. In order for there to be a reconciliation there has to have been an estrangement, right? Paul is saying that we messed up and had a falling out with God. But that was then. This is now.

He says we are back in a right relationship with God and the relationship doesn't look the way it used to look because *we* don't look the way we used to look. Because we're new creations it also means we are in new situations. So we must stop living our lives based on our old situations.

The next time someone talks crazy to you again, that's old situation language. I used to respond to in the old situation way. I don't respond in that way anymore. I don't even go there. I make the choice to respond in humility.

Change the script on that, brother. Change the script on that, sister. Running your mouth off hasn't worked yet. Nagging, fussing and complaining haven't worked yet. Why don't you try something different? You are in a new situation. Stop acting as if you were in the old one and reveal the new creature you are in Christ Jesus.

Real, authentic reconciliation does not happen by accident. Somebody has to step up to the plate and make it happen. So the text says, God the Father initiated the act of reconciliation by bringing us back to his face.

> *Now we have direct access to the very presence of God. We don't have to flee from His presence.*

In the old situation, we didn't have enough sense to go back to God. That's how stupid sin makes us. When we were swimming in sin and rebellion we didn't even know it. Some of us look back now and wonder how we could have done the things we did. Sin has a stupefying effect on us. That's why God by His grace had to reach down and snatch us out of the pit. If left to ourselves, we would have stayed down there, *stuck on stupid*.

So God has to be the initiator. I'm not trying to disparage our children but some of us need to see our children for what they are. Some of them are stuck on stupid and we need to go and get them.

God is the initiator of reconciliation. When Jesus Christ died on the cross in obedience to His Father, the Bible says the veil of the temple was torn in two. In other words, there was no more separation. Now we have direct access to the very presence of God. That is the good news of the gospel. We don't have to flee from His presence.

We will not have our character changed unless we live in the presence of the living God.

This is why we're no longer the same. We cannot be in the presence of the living God and remain the same. Some of you ask, how can somebody come to church every Sunday and still go out there and act the fool? What you don't get is that they attend church every Sunday but that's all they do. They come and get a taste of the presence of God but they are not living in His presence. We will not have our character changed unless we live in the presence of the living God. We can't just come for a taste.

So don't be fooled by folk who lift holy hands from 10 o'clock to 10:50 on Sunday, because Monday through Saturday it's a whole different story. But they've been in church for twenty years, you say. That's the problem. They been in the church of Christ for twenty years but Christ of the church has not truly been at work in them. Show me somebody in whom Christ of the church is at work and I will show you someone whose character and life have been changed—someone who has grasped the true meaning of reconciliation.

Reconciliation in Action

The veil has been torn so we can live in His presence, and that's where our change comes from. Fathers, do you want to see a change in your children? Then get them into your presence.

"But pastor, I'm always home!" you protest. "I don't go anywhere."

God doesn't have to bring Himself back. He never left. God is pulling us back to Himself.

However, we can be in the house without being present in the house. If all we do is lock ourselves in a room and channel surf from the Lakers' game to the Green Bay Packers, that's not being present in the house. Our presence means our influence and our covering. It means our voice is being heard. It means we are ordering the life of our children. They feel us there at the homework table. They know we're watching over them while they sleep. Sometimes I have to leave home before dawn, but before I walk out that door I go and visit every one of my children's rooms. And while they're asleep I put my hand on their heads and speak a quick prayer as I'm running out the door. They ought to know our presence is there in the house.

God is not reconciled to us. We are reconciled to God. He's been there the whole time. If the idea of reconciliation means to bring someone back, God doesn't have to bring Himself back. He never left. God is pulling us back to Himself. And parents, let me tell you—there is power in the pull. You want to see the lives and attitudes of your children change? Pull them back into a close relationship with you.

In the book of Jude, we read about those who are rebellious and those who stray. Jude says for some, be gentle and show kindness, while for others, snatch them by their garments. That is, some of us are too nice with our children. We need to grab them by the collar and pull them back to us!

God made things right between us and Him, not by ignoring the problem but by confronting it.

In order for this type of life-changing reconciliation to happen, God had to face sin head on. Look at 2 Corinthians 5:21: God made him who had no sin to be sin for us, so that in him we might become the righteousness of God (2 Corinthians 5:21 NIV).

In the Old Testament sin did not go away by people ignoring it. It had to be atoned for, through sacrifice and through death. So God the Father confronted the sin issue in our lives by making God the Son, who knew no sin, to become the perfect sacrifice on our behalf. God made things right between us and Him, not by ignoring the problem but by confronting it.

David missed a crucial opportunity of fatherhood by not confronting his issues head-on. Notice in our story that David brought his son to a house but not into his personal presence. He didn't understand that the boy didn't need a house—he needed a daddy.

Our sons don't need another car. They don't need another Nintendo or Gameboy or game player. They need their daddy.

Reconciliation must lead to restoration if it is going to work.

So David gave him a house. Remember, David was the king, so he would have owned all the property. He let Absalom stay in one of his houses but never let him back into his presence. He did not seek restoration.

Reconciliation Must Lead to Restoration

Reconciliation must lead to restoration if it is going to work. We have been reconciled by God to God. But notice that he does not stop there. Go to Ephesians 1:19-23 to be reminded of "his incomparably great power for us who believe."

> That power is the same as the mighty strength he exerted when he raised Christ from the dead and seated him at his right hand in the heavenly realms, far above all rule and authority,

> *power and dominion, and every name that is invoked, not only in the present age but also in the one to come. And God placed all things under his feet and appointed him to be head over everything for the church, which is his body, the fullness of him who fills everything in every way.* — **Ephesians 1:19-23 (NIV)**
>
> *As for you, you were dead in your transgressions and sins, in which you used to live when you followed the ways of this world and of the ruler of the kingdom of the air, the spirit who is now at work in those who are disobedient. All of us also lived among them at one time, gratifying the cravings of our flesh and following its desires and thoughts. Like the rest, we were by nature deserving of wrath. But because of his great love for us, God, who is rich in mercy, made us alive with Christ even when we were dead in transgressions—it is by grace you have been saved. And God raised us up with Christ and seated us with him in the heavenly realms in Christ Jesus...* — **Ephesians 2:1-6 (NIV)**

This is major for us as believers. It reveals the essence of what we are. Not only have we been reconciled to God, but now Paul says we have been positionally restored to His very presence. Paul wants us to understand the reality of our current position.

If the devil is at the feet of Jesus, and I'm in Christ, that means the devil is under my feet.

If you are a believer, if your name is written in the Book of Life, at this minute you are seated with Christ in the heavenly places. Your body may be down here but don't let the devil fool you. The reality is you are a citizen of heaven.

Every time you go through something you need to remember that you are currently seated with Christ. That means your mind has to be with Christ, your heart has to be with Christ, and your language has to come from a heavenly place. As believers, everything we do, we do from a heavenly position, from the presence of God. In God's restorative process he has made us alive with Christ and raised us up together with Christ, to sit with him in the heavenlies, above all principalities and powers. That's why I don't trip too much over the enemy. If the devil is under the feet of Jesus Christ and I'm in Christ, that means the devil is under my feet.

We have access to every resource that is available to Christ. Stop living beneath your privilege!

So not only are we in a position of authority over the enemy because we're in Christ. We also have access to every resource that is available to Christ. Paul says that we are joint heirs with Christ Jesus. Saints of God, stop living beneath your privilege! Everything that is available to Jesus Christ is available to you today. Greater is he that is in me than he that is in the world (1 John 4:4).

> But now in Christ Jesus you who once were far away have been brought near by the blood of Christ. For he himself is our peace, who has made the two groups one and has destroyed the

barrier, the dividing wall of hostility... — **Ephesians 2:13-14 (NIV)**

Just think about Absalom, stuck in that house. Do you see that half-hearted reconciliation and that zero restoration? There's so much power in reconciliation and restoration that it will change not only the situation but also the people in it.

Our inability to engage our children effectively when they are young will show itself in life-altering, destructive behavior when they are adults.

David brought Absalom back but for the most part he put him under house arrest. Parents, some of your children are asking how much longer you will keep making them pay for the mistakes they have made.

Let's go back to 2 Samuel 14:28-32.

Absalom lived two years in Jerusalem without seeing the king's face. Then Absalom sent for Joab in order to send him to the king, but Joab refused to come to him. So he sent a second time, but he refused to come. Then he said to his servants, "Look, Joab's field is next to mine, and he has barley there. Go and set it on fire." So Absalom's servants set the field on fire.

Then Joab did go to Absalom's house, and he said to him, "Why have your servants set my field on fire?"

Absalom said to Joab, "Look, I sent word to you and said, 'Come here so I can send you to the king to ask, "Why have I come from

> *Geshur? It would be better for me if I were still there!"" — 2 Samuel 14:28-32 (NIV)*

In other words, why do you have me here if you're not going to have me next to you? Why are you going to bring me all the way back from my grand-daddy's house where at least I was in the presence of a man who loved me? Why bring me back all the way here and then not engage me?

> *Now then, I want to see the king's face, and if I am guilty of anything, let him put me to death. — 2 Samuel 14:32 (NIV)*

He burns up a man's field. The distance and lack of connection forces Absalom to act out in a destructive way. The boy is yearning for his father and will do whatever is necessary to get the attention that he wants and needs. Listen to me, friends. Much of the destructive behavior we see in our children is a bitter fruit of the pain they are experiencing on the inside.

Don't miss the paradox here. Absalom is David's child but Absalom is a grown man, which makes him even more dangerous. Our inability to engage our children effectively when they are young will show itself in life-altering, destructive behavior when they are adults. What is our child trying to communicate to us with their behavior? Why is our grown child still using adolescent methods to address their issues of hurt and pain?

This man burns up another person's field, all to get the attention of his father. What more does your child have to do to say he needs you in his life? And the fact that he's behaving crazy, especially if he's grown up but doing childish things, means he needs a mamma and a daddy to deal with the childishness that remains inside of him.

It's time to set the house in order. It's time for children to honor their parents. It's time for husbands to cover their wives and children.

We can ignore it if we want to. But with adult children we're in a more challenging position. How do we deal with our adult children? The rule of Pastor Jody and the rule of his house, as I mentioned before, is that while our adult children are living in our house we have a right to speak to them and correct them.

It's time to set the house in order. It's time for children to honor their parents. It's time for husbands to cover their wives and children. If you're now an empty nester, pocket these principles for your grandchildren and for your adult children as they raise their own kids.

In chapter two, we read of the spiraling effect of David's missed opportunities. He had opportunities to step in as a father and he did not do so.

Remember, David had sent for Absalom to come out of exile and come to Jerusalem but then he said he didn't want to see him.

"Put him in his own house. I don't want to see his face."

We called this a half-hearted reconciliation and zero restoration. So Absalom was living in his house and never seeing his father David, and finally he began to act out. He burned up Joab's field in an effort to get attention, and told Joab he wanted to come into his daddy's presence.

> So Joab went to the king and told him this. Then the king summoned Absalom, and he came in and bowed down with his face to the ground before the king. And the king kissed Absalom.
> — *2 Samuel 14:33 (NIV)*

It looked as if everything was fine now. Absalom got his wish. He came back into the king's presence. He bowed before the king, and the king kissed him—another sign of reconciliation between father and son. Everything looked hunky dory.

> After this Absalom got himself a chariot and horses, and fifty men to run before him. — *2 Samuel 15:1 (ESV)*

The writer is telling us what happened after the reconciliation, after the embrace. Absalom went and armed himself. Although there was reconciliation, there was still too much damage to the relationship for there to be a true and authentic repair or restoration.

A Changed Relationship

Authentic reconciliation should always lead to reparation. If your relationship still looks like it did before the reconciliation, you either had a half-hearted reconciliation or a fake one. Some relationships use terminology indicative of reconciliation. Nevertheless, the fruit of the relationship, as it should be, is never on display. In other words, if you say everything is cool, then why isn't the relationship fixed?

Some of us are spending our energy trying to repair a relationship when God is telling us we can't do it in our own strength.

Some relationships can never be repaired unless God does the repairing for us. Some of us are spending our energy trying to repair a relationship when God is telling us we can't do it in our own strength. And some of us are expending much of our emotional capital trying to repair a relationship that God doesn't want repaired in the first place. God says it's broken for a reason, and he's not going to fix it. We need to stop trying to resurrect something that is dead. That's why for some it's easier just to walk away.

I wish that I could tell you that there is something redemptive about this story of David and Absalom, but I can't. Nothing good comes out of it. There was too much damage and everyone was affected in a major way.

Let me tell you what happened. David was running when a man from the house of Saul kicked him and cursed him out.

> So David and his men continued along the road while Shimei was going along the hillside opposite him, cursing as he went and throwing stones at him and showering him with dirt. The king and all the people with him arrived at their destination exhausted. And there he refreshed himself. — **2 Samuel 16:13-14 (NIV)**

So there it is. David was running, and a man was throwing rocks at him. This was the king! Since he was running his eyes were open and his mouth probably was too. The man was kicking dust at him, so David was coughing and hacking as he struggled to reach his destination. The text tells us that when he finally arrived he was so weary he needed to be refreshed.

The enemy has a way of knowing how to kick us when we're down.

Did you know the enemy has a way of knowing how to kick us when we're down? He will send people to us who ought to refresh us and they'll curse us and kick dust at us. And it's just to set us up for a kill! Because if the devil can wear us down spiritually, when he's ready to give us the knock-out punch, we won't have the strength to pray or to fast. Nor do we have the strength to stand for what we need to stand for.

We need to be careful of who we allow in our space when we are going through a rough time. Are they helping us or just kicking dust down our throat?

> *Then the Cushite arrived and said, "My lord the king, hear the good news! The Lord has vindicated you today by delivering you from the hand of all who rose up against you."*
>
> *The king asked the Cushite, "Is the young man Absalom safe?"*
>
> *The Cushite replied, "May the enemies of my lord the king and all who rise up to harm you be like that young man."*
>
> *The king was shaken. He went up to the room over the gateway and wept. As he went, he said: "O my son Absalom! My son, my son Absalom! If only I had died instead of you—O Absalom, my son, my son!"* — **2 Samuel 18:31-33 (NIV)**

Absalom had been killed. But look at 2 Samuel 18:5.

> *And the king ordered Joab and Abishai and Ittai, 'Deal gently for my sake with the young man Absalom.' And all the people heard when the king gave orders to all the commanders about Absalom.* — **2 Samuel 18:5 (ESV)**

Even though Absalom had done all this to his daddy, David had still instructed his men to deal gently with him. His heart was still knitted to his son. Listen, my friends, don't ever let the pain of your children who hurt you get so deep inside of you that you still can't wish them well.

Absalom had betrayed his father. As the prophet Nathan prophesied to David, what the king had done in secret with Bathsheba would be done to him in broad daylight before all Israel (2 Samuel 12:11-12). Absalom had slept with David's wives (2 Samuel 16:22), and when he finally returned to Jerusalem, David shut those wives away for the rest of their lives (2 Samuel 20:3). He would never return to them again, all because of Absalom. Yet despite all this, he instructed his soldiers to deal gently with his son.

The ability to seek out God in humility and connect with your children leads to authentic reconciliation.

Part of being a good father is knowing when to be merciful and not allowing your pain to be so acute that you cannot show mercy to your children. Through his pain, David still attempted gentleness, but ultimately we see no clear, authentic reconciliation between David and his son.

The Discipline of a Father

In contrast to David's responses, let us turn to Hosea, chapter 11. Fathers, hear this carefully. In your DNA is the ability to do everything that we've talked about in this book. It's the ability to seek out God in humility, connect with your children, engage your children, be intimate with your children, and deal with your children. All this leads to authentic reconciliation.

In Hosea 11, God is talking to Israel as a father.

> When Israel was a child, I loved him, and out of Egypt I called my son. The more they were called, the more they went away. They kept sacrificing to the Baals and burning offerings to idols. Yet it was I who taught Ephraim to walk; I took them up by the arms...
> — *Hosea 11:1-3 (ESV)*

This is a daddy talking. In our culture we normally see the mother doing this, but here is God talking like a daddy.

> I took them up by their arms, but they did not know that I healed them. — *Hosea 11:3 (ESV)*

This is still the daddy talking.

> I led them with cords of human kindness, with the bands of love, and I lifted the yoke from their neck and bent down to feed them. They shall not return to the land of Egypt, but Assyria shall be their king because they have refused to return to me. — *Hosea 11:4-5 (ESV)*

This is the discipline of a father.

> The sword shall rage against their cities, consume the bars of their gates, and put an end to their plans. My people are determined to turn from me, and though they call out to the Most High, he will not raise them up at all. — **Hosea 11:6-7 (ESV)**

Now we come to verse 8, one of my favorite verses in all of Scripture:

> How can I give you up, Ephraim? How can I hand you over, Israel? How can I treat you like Admah? How can I make you like Zeboiim? My heart recoils within me; all my compassion is aroused. — **Hosea 11:8 (ESV)**

This is a daddy talking again. Who has a wayward son right now? Who has a wayward daughter? Who has children in rebellion? God as a father is talking to his children, and that same spirit is in us. We have the same ability to connect.

> I led them with cords of kindness, with the bands of love... — **Hosea 11:4 (ESV)**

This depicts a child being led by something around their neck but not an oppressive cord. It is a cord of gentleness, a cord of love and compassion. But it is still a cord for leading the child. "Oh, how can I give you up?" the Lord says. "How can I turn My back on you? My compassion grows warm and tender within me, even though you are a rebellious nation" (Hosea 11:8). We see here a picture of that "ornament of grace" of which Charles Swindoll spoke.

In Romans 2:4 we read:

> *Or do you despise the riches of His kindness, restraint, and patience, not recognizing that God's kindness is intended to lead you to repentance?* — **Romans 2:4**

Therefore, it is God's kindness that leads us towards repentance. In other words, "Even when you're out there acting stupid, I'm still blessing you and providing for you. I'm still putting food on your table. When everybody else got laid off, you still had a job and a car to drive. You've got your health and a roof over your head. You still have clothes on your back and friends to talk to. You still have family members in your life. Despite everything you've done, I continue to bless you.

"And I will keep blessing you. I will keep providing for you and loving you and prospering you. And at some point in time, my goodness ought to wake you up. It ought to make you say, 'I can't keep acting like this against a God who shows me so much love and compassion.'"

The book of Hosea shows us what authentic reconciliation looks like. It is a father called to action, engaging with his kids, seeking reconciliation, and enjoying a changed relationship. This is what David missed, even though he was a man after God's heart. But true reconciliation remains ours to experience.

WORKBOOK

Chapter 3 Questions

Question: Many of us miss opportunities, not because of a lack of discernment but because we're not paying attention. How will you respond differently to your family members? How can you better focus on opportunities to bring your family together and shape their lives?

_____
_____
_____
_____
_____
_____
_____
_____
_____
_____
_____

Question: Real, authentic reconciliation does not happen by accident. What specific steps will you take to seek authentic reconciliation with a friend or loved one? What is holding you back?

_____
_____
_____
_____
_____
_____
_____
_____
_____
_____

Question: We will not have our character changed unless we live in the presence of the living God. How will you begin seeking reconciliation with God? In what ways will you change the way you live in His presence?

_____
_____
_____
_____
_____
_____
_____
_____

Question: Some relationships can never be repaired unless God does the repairing for us. If you ask God for help in restoring a relationship, what will you do while you are waiting? When is it acceptable to walk away from a relationship?

Question: What is the hardest thing for you about seeking God? Do you find it easy to accept His grace? Why or why not? What is the most important lesson you will take away from this book?

_____
_____
_____
_____
_____
_____
_____

Action: We need to be able to discern those pivotal situations that could reshape the landscape of our family. Pay attention to those around you so you can be tuned in to potential problems. Remember, every time you go through something, you are seated with Christ. In prayerful consideration, ask God to help you restore any relationships. Seek out God in humility, connect with your family, and engage your children. Just do it!

Chapter 3 Notes

CONCLUSION

Grace to Move Forward

We've just finished reading about David—a man who mirrored God's own heart. God chose David for his humility and what He saw in him. We may not completely understand why God chose David because we do not understand David's heart as God did. Yet, we also saw many of David's ugly mistakes.

From David's humble beginnings to the tragic consequences of his sins, we journeyed with him and learned how we can seek out God in humility, engage our families, and enjoy authentic reconciliation. We can avoid the same types of mistakes in our lives with our families as we move forward in accordance with God's design.

All of us have made mistakes and bad decisions in our lives. We've all taken wrong turns and fallen flat on our faces, and we still screw up at times. But that does not keep us from being everything God has called us to be. What He declares about our life will come to pass.

Thus, God allows us to make mistakes. God already knows the mistakes we or our family members will make. He has a plan to correct those mistakes and lead us to reconciliation. That plan includes stepping up and strengthening our families by taking action and engaging family members when they aren't perfect. The eventual goal is reconciliation, through which our relationships are improved. By God's grace we seek His reconciliation. By this reconciliation, we are free and can relate to our families.

If we want to be people after God's own heart, we must obey God, actively engage with our families, and have a heart for authentic reconciliation.

While David made significant mistakes, we need to understand that with all of his faults and failures—and there were plenty—he was still the greatest king Israel had ever known. Having David as king was still part of God's plan.

As we now understand why God favored David's humility, we also saw that if we want to be people who reflect God's own heart, we must obey Him, actively engage with our families, and have a heart for authentic reconciliation with God and others. God gives us the grace to do this.

GOD'S WILL > YOUR PLAN

God has a plan and a purpose
—and you are a part of it!

Discover what the story of Jonah can teach you about embracing your call, purpose, and identity.

About the Author

Educated at Talbot School of Theology, Jody D. Moore currently serves as the Senior Pastor-Teacher at Praise Tabernacle Bible Church in the City of Chino, California. He has held executive leadership roles both in ministry and in several Fortune 500 companies. He specializes in leadership development and organizational assessment. He has served on the boards of several non-profits. He is the author of *God's Will>Your Plan* and currently blogs at www.theironsharpener.com. Pastor Jody resides in Southern California with his wife and three daughters.

About Sermon To Book

SermonToBook.com began with a simple belief: that sermons should be touching lives, *not* collecting dust. That's why we turn sermons into high-quality books that are accessible to people all over the globe.

Turning your sermon series into a book exposes more people to God's Word, better equips you for counseling, accelerates future sermon prep, adds credibility to your ministry, and even helps make ends meet during tight times.

John 21:25 tells us that the world itself couldn't contain the books that would be written about the work of Jesus Christ. Our mission is to try anyway. Because, in Heaven, there will no longer be a need for sermons or books. Our time is now.

If God so leads you, we'd love to work with you on your sermon or sermon series.

Visit www.sermontobook.com to learn more.

www.ingramcontent.com/pod-product-compliance
Lightning Source LLC
Chambersburg PA
CBHW070609050426
42450CB00011B/3022